A HOARD FOR WINTER

A Hoard for Winter

VIRGINIA C. GILDERSLEEVE

COLUMBIA UNIVERSITY PRESS

NEW YORK AND LONDON 1962

The frontispiece is a portrait by Harold Brett, July, 1955
Photographed by the Kelsey Studio
Copyright © 1962 Columbia University Press
Library of Congress Catalog Card Number: 62-20310
"Calling All Women!" © 1957 The Curtis Publishing Company
Reproduced by permission

TO MY

seven thousand Barnard daughters

WITH AFFECTION AND GOOD WISHES

PREFACE

A FTER I retired from Barnard in 1947, I lived for fifteen years with Elizabeth Reynard, '22, in happy companionship. Though grimly afflicted with recurrent physical ills, we were both able at times to do some writing and each of us naturally took an intense interest in the other's work. My autobiography, *Many A Good Crusade*, published in 1954, provided us with a great deal of entertainment. Pulling around from a bad heart attack after that, I slowly began to write again, and over the next seven years produced a number of essays. I enjoyed writing them and they gave E. R. much pleasure. She thought other Barnard graduates of my time might also like to see what their Dean had been thinking about in her retirement. So she left in her will, when she died in 1962, a sum of money to cover the cost of publication and distribution to alumnae. Hence this book. I greatly doubt whether it is worthy of her warm regard.

The little collection offers a considerable variety of subject. Some essays deal with grave problems of the moment that lower threateningly over us. They were touched off by the news of the day which batters us through press, radio, television, and magazine, and which often reawakens in me knowledge, interests, and visions of my past. A few of the essays turn back to personalities of bygone years, in the fascinating historical pastime of seeking to sense what the world was like to people of long ago. And in a very few I have let my fancy wander to ideas even more remote. It is odd that two of my chief pleasures—music and archaeology—are by chance not represented.

A number of the essays here included have already been printed in various publications, as is duly noted. But some, including those that E. R. liked best, have not hitherto been published.

Any unity that the book possesses arises from the fact that all the articles were written in the years when my age was 75 to 82. I like to think that the modest collection offers, therefore, one answer to a question much discussed nowadays, when science has so greatly prolonged, sometimes unfortunately, the span of human life: How can the aged occupy themselves when they must perforce withdraw from their active work in the world; especially if they are so crippled as to make physical pastimes impossible, even weeding the lawn or knitting?

The answer is that we have to occupy ourselves mostly with our minds. This is difficult if we have not already accumulated during our active years, as I happily did, a good store of various interests—really diverse and widespread—to draw upon, to read about, to think about, to talk about, perhaps to write about. The process is much like the Social Security System: you pay in during your early and middle life and then you have a support to lean on in your time of need. Or, to use a more picturesque simile, you build up through the summer a hoard of seeds and nuts and acorns and other toothsome bits, as I see the grey squirrels doing so smartly and busily beside our house, and there is a rich store to draw upon when the snows of winter block the paths and the bitter winds whistle about your snug nest.

VIRGINIA C. GILDERSLEEVE
"Navarre," Bedford Village, New York, March, 1962

CONTENTS

THE ABUSE OF DEMOCRACY

✽ ✽ Written in 1956 and published in the *Saturday Review* of November 24, 1956. This essay contains in brief the main points of my lifelong credo of scholarship and education. I had been preaching them for many years but in the flabby state afflicting American education they seemed in 1956 quite startling. "Provocative" several comments called the article. Less than a year after its publication the Sputniks circled the globe and instantly a great chorus of Americans burst forth in criticisms far more violent and comprehensive than mine. So that my essay now (1958) sounds rather obvious. Will it when it is read a few years hence? Or will American education have relapsed happily into easygoing flabbiness?

EDUCATION in our country has been harmed as well as helped by the word "democracy." That chameleon-like word, which means so many different things to so many different people (witness the interpretations the Russians put upon it!), arouses emotions everywhere. We Americans would lay down our lives for the meaning which we devoutly believe in and value. We ought to lay down, if not our lives, at least a good barrage against the twisted meaning and misuse of it that threatens to wreck the quality of our education.

"Democracy" is fundamentally a *political* term, applying to political units or groups of human beings. We follow democratic principles, I hope, in the government of our nation, our state, our city, and the little village in which I live. But when we begin to apply "democracy" in the fields of education or scholarship grave perils descend upon us.

One of these perils is the fetish of the majority vote. In operating any political government we have to depend upon a vote to determine what policies are to be adopted, what persons elected to represent us and carry out those policies. The majority, under limitations imposed by the Constitution and the courts, must determine these things. It is a convenient way of settling political action. We have not been able to find a better one.

The peril is that this useful device for settling political matters comes to be regarded by people at large with a kind of superstitious reverence, as if a majority vote could settle the *truth* of a theory or proposition in the field of scholarship or education. A few moments' serious thought will convince anyone that even the most august convention, the wisest meeting of the Parent-Teacher Association, or of the American Legion, even of the Senate of the United States, cannot by majority vote determine the truth or the falsity of, let us say, the latest Einstein theory. That has to be decided in the long run by the innumerable tests of time and experiment. Even for questions far less abstruse and complex than the Einstein theory, truth or falsity must be weighed and determined by the politically indifferent scales of time.

To a lesser degree this is true not only of the scholar's

search for truth but also of matters of educational policy. Yet we have to settle a good many questions in schools and colleges and universities, important questions of educational policy such as the requirements of the curriculum, by a majority vote of the faculty under the safeguards of parliamentary law. Yet we should never forget that this cannot possibly establish their verity or wisdom; the decisions should always be open to later reconsideration and further discussion.

In the fields of scholarship and education it is also important to remember that popular opinion polls or the majority votes of school boards, trustees, or legislative bodies cannot determine the ultimate *value* of the research project or the educational method or aim. Even Research Councils, though they have to decide what projects to aid, cannot really determine this. The greatest possible freedom should be given to the young scholar to pursue the truth in whatever field interests him, however useless it may appear to the public at large or even to smaller groups of experts. I was immensely impressed in my youth by that remarkable book *The Life of Louis Pasteur*, by Vallery-Radot. The early portion tells how the young Pasteur spent the first years of his scientific research studying racemic acid, in particular the peculiarities of the left-handed and right-handed crystals of racemic acid. Nothing could seem more foolish to the average citizen than to have a promising young man waste his time in this obscure and apparently useless research. And yet, apart from adding to man's total knowledge of truth, Pasteur's researches in the long run were to have stupendous practical value, saving the lives of thousands of human beings and billions of francs for the silk industry of France.

Another instance of the apparent uselessness of scholarly research impressed me deeply in my early years. There was a professor of zoology at Columbia who, as a hobby, studied medieval armor. He became a curator of medieval armor at the Metropolitan Museum of Art in New York. His detailed studies of this subject seemed a pleasant and harmless diversion but, oh, so useless in the early 1900s. Then suddenly came World War I, a change in methods of warfare, and the urgent need once again for armor. Professor Bashford Dean was called from his laboratories and his museum halls by the Ordnance Department of the Army to design helmets for our soldiers in trench warfare.

To me any addition to man's knowledge of truth, either positive or negative, seems to make a piece of research thoroughly worthwhile. But apart from that it may ultimately, like Pasteur's work and Professor Bashford Dean's, prove of great practical usefulness. We simply cannot tell. We must be very careful not to let public-opinion polls or majority votes block the search for truth in any field.

Of late years it has become increasingly difficult to give the young scholar a chance to adventure into his chosen field because so much research now has to be carried on by "teams" and with the help of expensive scientific apparatus such as computers. Of course, the allocation of sums of money for these purposes must be determined by some responsible board or committee or council conversant with such problems, and these may sometimes discourage eccentric new experiments. Recalling a wise and kindly lady who many years ago used to give me an annual gift to be used to help what we called "the undeserving poor," meaning students who were ineligible for any scholarship or even grant-in-aid, but who somehow seemed worth taking a chance on, I wonder whether it might not be a good idea for some imaginative millionaire to establish a fund to be used to assist researchers in what seemed to practically everybody else wild and useless projects?

I recall one rather quaint result of trying to apply that eminently useful political device, the majority vote, in the conduct of college affairs. Fired by enthusiasm for democracy, some of the more radical students in many colleges began to think of the college as a political unit and of themselves as citizens, entitled, according to the proper democratic process, to determine the conduct of the affairs of the institution by majority vote of the student body or some specialized organizations like political clubs. This was especially likely to arise in the cases of invitations that some students wanted to extend to highly sensational speakers from outside to come and use the college campus as a sounding board. Then any interference by the administration or faculty would be condemned as a violation of that right to "freedom of speech" guaranteed to American citizens by our Constitution. Or any objections by the college authorities to offensive and perhaps libelous matter printed in a student publication would be condemned as a violation of the sacred democratic right to "freedom of the press." Now I have always been perfectly sure that in a college no such rights existed for students as students. The only right a student has *as a student* is the right to receive the best possible education that the college can give. (He retains of course his political rights as a citizen of the state.)

When I expounded this view of mine to the students of Barnard College at Columbia University in the City of New York, as I frequently did during my term of thirty-six years as Dean, some of them used to look a bit startled at first, as if I were advancing some shockingly undemocratic idea. But I generally convinced most of them of the soundness of my thesis when I pointed out that the Trustees and under them the Faculty, according to a charter granted by the Board of Regents of the State of New York, were responsible for the operation of the college and would be held responsible by law, by community opinion, and especially by the parents of the students, for anything that occurred in the college.

Knowing that they will ultimately be held responsible for anything the students may do, it is the function of the faculty and the administration to decide what measure of self-government or student government conduces to good education. Should the faculty think, I often pointed out, that a stern disciplinary regime, like that at West Point, would be most effective educationally for the good of the students, then it would be the duty of the faculty to impose some such regime. If, on the other hand, they thought that a considerable measure of self-government, the carrying of really serious responsibility by the students in managing college affairs, especially extracurricular ones, gave them experience of real educational value, then obviously it was the duty of the faculty to delegate the largest possible measure of self-government, freedom of speech, and freedom of the student press conducive to these educational ends; not because these things were the "rights" of citizens in a political unit under our democratic form of government, but because they were good for the development of the minds and characters of the undergraduates. On the basis of this policy the faculty and the administration of Barnard College, as I knew it, gave, and I imagine still does, very great power and responsibility to student government. Moreover, we always encouraged free criticism by the students of the curriculum and the administration of the college, asking only that comments and suggestions for improvement should be presented in a courteous manner.

It seemed to me that self-government worked admirably among our students and gave them experience which in later life proved valuable to them as they participated as citizens in the political government of our democratic republic. And I think we always got on better because we had analyzed just what the "rights" were and where the final responsibility lay.

In my time at Barnard College we had on the whole a lively, independent, and courageous student body—eager to speak up and express their views and try to make them prevail, containing a small number of Marxists and other extremists, enough to provide some spicy controversies. And

I always wanted to keep them like this. Today I imagine college students may be less bold, less full of original initiative under the lingering influence of McCarthyism, apprehensive lest some innocent sophomore membership in a socialist club may stand as a blot on their record throughout their lives and cut them off from advancement and success. I trust that these sad days will pass.

There is a somewhat different use of the word "democratic" which I do not wish to condemn: the application of it to the social atmosphere of a college. According to our American ideals it is of course highly desirable that the social atmosphere should be essentially "democratic"; by this we mean that just as far as possible every student should be judged by her own character, personality, and ability, quite irrespective of the background from which she comes. It is a wonderful feeling to find oneself in a small community standing entirely on one's own feet, knowing almost nothing of the families and the social backgrounds of one's fellow Americans and judging them entirely on their own individual merits. They will vary immensely of course and will have been deeply influenced by the backgrounds from which they came. But to a considerable extent, if the college gets a good start, it can achieve for its students on the personal and social side a measure of equality of opportunity.

All that I have been saying is comparatively unimportant when contrasted with the very gravest of the perils which the misunderstanding and abuse of the term democracy has brought upon the country. This is the idea that it is undemocratic to give better educational opportunities to better people. By better people I mean individuals equipped with better brains or better characters or both than the majority of the community.

Democracy is an idealistic form of government, highly desirable and highly difficult to operate. For its success it needs a fairly informed and sensible citizenry. Education must be universal. Every boy and girl is to have a vote in elections. So every boy and girl, as well as some useful technical training, must have as much general education as he or she can absorb.

Even more important for the survival of democracy than a well-informed general citizenry—and this is my crucial point—is the possession of good leaders. These leaders must have trained minds and sound principles and must provide highly developed special skills in many fields. We need them most of all perhaps in politics and statesmanship, but the recent alarmed clamor over our extreme shortage of engineers shows some realization of our perilous situation. We simply must increase greatly our supply of leaders and experts to meet the challenges of the intricately complex, many-sided problems of the world of today. Our present shortage is due in large part to a false idea of democracy, the strange notion that good things that can't be had by everybody should not be had by anybody.

Leaders and experts generally need the equivalent not only of a sound secondary education, but of full college training and, in most cases, years of advanced graduate or professional study beyond that. (Several of our finest leaders have had none of these!) Now the average American is simply not qualified and cannot be trained to absorb a standard college education. We might as well face that fact frankly. We must sift out from the general mass of pupils in our schools the minority who show promise of being able to absorb the education necessary for political leadership, for atomic physics, for the work of teachers, physicians, historians, philosophers, and a multitude of other much needed experts. We must sift them out by the wisest and fairest tests we can devise and the judgment of their teachers; free them from the hampering mass of the intellectually inferior students and those unwilling to learn, and give to these most promising candidates the best possible teaching, the best opportunities for development of mind, knowledge, and character.

I never realized how shocking such a simple and, to me, obviously essential procedure seemed to many of my fellow educators until I went in 1946 on the U.S. Education Mission to Japan to advise the new Japanese democracy regarding the reorganization of their educational system. The members of our Mission were sharply divided on this question of selection of pupils for the continuing of education. One considerable group of our experts believed it highly undemocratic, vicious, and poisonous to apply any tests to candidates in order to select the most promising few. This point of view was advanced, to my great amazement, by the City Superintendent of Schools of one of our great cities. *All* pupils should have the same opportunities, he felt. You should never test them to find out whether some of them had better brains than others. The only way to choose students for further education, he said, was by a sort of picking by lot. If, for example, you had only five vacancies in a high school and there were ten applicants, then you should take all the odd numbers on the list. It would be very undemocratic to apply any sort of test to see whether five of them had better brains and more ambition and interest than the others. He really did say that. It's hard to believe, but it was so.

I gather that this school of thought among the educators believes that every American child, whatever his brains, his interests, his desire to study, or his indifference and laziness, should be put through high school and junior college even if this should result in the curtailing of opportunities for the really able and ambitious students to go on and prepare for leadership and special professional or scientific skills.

Picking out the best students, those capable of further development which might be of great use to their country, is made even more difficult than need be by the strange new practice of forbidding marks and forcing teachers and principals to promote pupils, even if they have failed lamentably in the year's work. Marking some students "Excellent" and others "Failed" is said to be a highly undemocratic practice. Besides which, marks, some of the psychiatrists tell us, impair the good relations between the children and their parents. As for promoting some members of the class and obliging others, who through lack of ability or through sheer idleness have failed to register any sort of achievement, to repeat the year's work, that, they consider, is obviously a highly undemocratic procedure—"discrimination."

Thus, the unfortunate teachers are deprived of some of the most useful tools of instruction and discipline, and the pupils are deprived of the valuable knowledge of how they rate in comparison with their fellows.

When we began to set up in our colleges special honors courses for the better students, designed to give them opportunities for more rapid and extensive development than the average group, there were shrill cries of "discrimination" and "undemocratic action." In schools, we are told, arranging special sections for the more promising pupils and segregating the lazy or incompetent ones in another class arouses loud protests from parents who insist that their children must not be put into a group known to be intended for "dummies."

We must break down this state of mind if our democracy is to survive. Can we not somehow put brain power on the same basis as physical powers or other special talents? As Dean Jacques Barzun of Columbia University said recently, "As regards familiar and especially physical powers, the public understands that there can be no claims, no rights, except those of ability. You do not get your turn at leading the band if you are deaf to music. . . . The plea for the recognition of brains must be granted."

If the statisticians are right there will be, some ten or fifteen years from now, twice as many students in the colleges. We have not now nearly enough good teachers for the present enrollment. Where can we possibly get enough for the additional three million? Television may help a little, but cannot really meet the need. (I should like to deal with that subject in another essay.)

It is obvious that, far more than we now do, we should shed many of the students who are clogging the upper grades. They must be provided with technical training if they are qualified and will apply themselves to it. Ample "adult education" opportunities should be available for those who wake up mentally and morally later in life. But to keep boys and girls, irrespective of their ability and interest, on through the upper years of regular high school and the first year or two in college seems a waste of effort and resources. And does it do them any good? The present record of some of our teenagers seems to make that doubtful.

Surely many of these young people should leave school and go to work in paid jobs. They would then be less frustrated, happier, and more useful to the community. Later on some of them as adults will realize the desirability of more education and want it. They should then be given every opportunity their ability merits, and out of this group will come ultimately a few of our most brilliant minds.

If many who are now allowed to continue should be weeded out, it is on the other hand equally true that a large number of students who ought to go on to college, whose minds and characters warrant further education, do not get these opportunities. That is an immensely important problem with which we must grapple more effectively than we do now. There must have been, even in this prosperous and kindly country, many boys and girls of talent and character who faced obstacles like those over which, for example, Booker T. Washington and George W. Carver triumphed, but who through lack of determination and good fortune failed to win a chance for that development of their gifts which would have made them as useful to their country as those two remarkable citizens.

The brains and the potential leadership of our youth are the most precious assets of the nation. We must seek them out wherever they may be and try to make sure, as far as is humanly possible, that poverty, social obscurity, physical handicaps, or slow development do not keep them from rising to their full maturity. Having found them, let us then put them through a sound and vigorous training which is not hampered by the mass of incompetents and idlers.

From whatever source they come, we must cherish and develop our best, for democracy needs them if it is to survive. Otherwise, in the name of that form of government and of life which we are trying to preserve, here in America we may kill it.

OUR EXPENDABLE WORLD

⚘⚘ Written in 1958, for obvious reasons.

I T was William L. White's book *They Were Expendable* that first started the general use of this word. In war it applied to men or ships or machines that could be easily dispensed with, could be without scruple sacrificed to secure some advantage, even a small advantage. Not a pleasant idea for the "expendable" ones, if they were human, not a satisfactory end to anticipate, just being something of little value that could be thrown away without any sense of serious loss. Yet during World War II many thousands of men were "expendable"—and were expended.

Things as well as men, things that used to be highly valued and cherished, have during recent years become more and more expendable. On Manhattan Island, for example, buildings are especially expendable. I can remember vividly that not long ago "the mile and a half of millionaires" lined upper Fifth Avenue east of Central Park. They were residences of the very rich, on which had been lavished all the best that the age knew of architecture and its kindred arts, all that money could buy of beauty from America, Europe, the Orient. They are gone now, practically all demolished to make room for great bastions of apartment houses.

Similarly, many a hotel or office building has been destroyed, to be replaced by a new structure which will produce more income. Land is scarce and valuable on Manhattan. Buildings are expendable.

How does that affect the creative mind of the architect, I wonder? The men who planned and so lovingly erected the Parthenon or the Cathedral at Chartres felt confident that these creations of their spirit and skill would stand for centuries, preserving for their builders at least a bit of immortality in a world of change. But now, any new structure in New York may go to the scrap heap in thirty years or so. Perhaps that is why the architects of today are tediously copying each other.

Even for supposedly permanent monuments their fate is uncertain. I knew the young architect who fifty years ago won the competition for the design of the Soldiers and Sailors Monument which was erected at that glorious site on Riverside Drive, to commemorate forever the heroism of our fighting men. I watched it begin to crumble away and weaken badly, until the public had to be kept at a distance from it lest they be injured by its collapsing marble. Years passed and it seemed impossible to get the City Council to appropriate money to repair and preserve it.

Has the public cared? Only an occasional voice has been raised; the vast majority of New Yorkers are too deeply infected with the current slogan: "Throw it away and get a new one!" They seem quite willing to see the debris carted to the dump. I am glad young Charlie Stoughton could not foresee the future when he proudly won that competition.

As our American way of life becomes more and more mechanized, as personal labor becomes more and more expensive and tiresome or boring, as domestic service becomes practically unobtainable, "expendability" spreads to many of our once cherished possessions. We used proudly to inherit beautiful table and bed linen which had belonged to our grandmothers and been tenderly laundered and cared for over the years. Now a brief spell of washing machines, bleaches, and detergents swiftly demolishes the fine fabrics and we take to paper napkins—even paper sheets, I hear— which can be just thrown away.

A friend of mine who used to teach a large class in American Literature at Barnard College tried a few years ago an experiment in the psychological attraction of expendability. She asked the young women if, when they were married and had homes of their own, they would prefer to have beautiful and valuable eighteenth century furniture, which had to be cared for (no dirty feet up on upholstery, or hot plates or cocktail glasses on tabletops!), rather than ordinary cheap modern furniture which you didn't have to worry about, but could throw away and replace when it got too dilapidated. Out of a class of one hundred only a scant half-dozen hands were raised in favor of eighteenth century elegance. The modern young American preferred a carefree life with possessions that could be easily replaced by machine made substitutes.

More and more our private lives will lack, I perceive,

beautiful and delicate things. To see them we shall have to go to museums. There, the lovely objects from the past will not be really alive, serving their natural function, but at least they will not for a long time, I trust, become expendable.

In an age of machines it is natural and inevitable that many of our useful possessions should be expendable, for machines wear out and must be replaced. The automobile, the machine which is the present ruling passion of Americans, as well as their indispensable servitor now that busses and railway trains are so rapidly fading from the countryside, is an interesting example of expendability greatly increased by a really terrific pressure of advertising and a yearning for social status. Though "planned obsolescence," one of our latest devices for expendability, is deliberately built into them, the family cars could often be perfectly adequate for years beyond the date at which the owners succumb to the wiles and lures of the commercials. "Turn it in and get an up-to-date model!" And the irresistible inclination to keep up with the Joneses is never finally satisfied until it achieves a Cadillac.

The terrible age in which we live, with its memories of recent hideous wars and its constant threat of more hideous ones to come, has greatly increased our American tendency to regard things as expendable. The armaments race has forced us to devote nearly a third of our vast industrial system to the production of machines and materials intended to be expended swiftly—exploded or destroyed if there is a war in the next year or two, obsolete, scrapped, and replaced if the war is deferred until a bit later. It is arresting to realize that if by some heaven-sent miracle peace could be guaranteed tomorrow, the country would collapse in the worst of depressions. So closely is our economy tied to the machinery of destruction and death.

Human life also, in these strange times, often seems to be expendable, and expendable on a huge scale. It is odd to say this of an era when the individual is so widely cherished and preserved. Medical science has cured so many human ills, it has prolonged the life expectancy by many years, it even keeps the sick and the aged alive for long spans of time when death would seem more merciful. Gallant efforts are made by organized society to eliminate hunger, poverty, human suffering of every kind, to rescue the desolate orphan, to reform the young delinquent.

Yet our modern American attitude toward human life is strangely ambivalent. We tolerate the sacrifice of thousands of lives by motor accidents on our roads, and encourage the makers to build cars larger, faster, more dangerous. We are even becoming accustomed to the idea of the massacre of great numbers of people—not just soldiers and sailors and airmen in battle but thousands on thousands of civilians, men, women, and children, annihilated in their own homes or at their peaceful daily work. I saw the devastated stretches of London, where so many died. I lived for a month in the wreckage of the great city of Tokyo, 85 percent destroyed by us, with more than 100,000 of its citizens. When we dropped the atomic bombs on Hiroshima and Nagasaki we created a dreadful precedent. Whole cities with all who live therein are now expendable: in the twinkling of an eye they may be blown to dust.

Yes, our minds are really growing used to the idea of this vast expendability. And so rapidly has scientific skill increased the size and the deadliness of these weapons that we can now conceive the destruction of a whole nation, a continent, or even the globe itself. I read occasionally in the newspapers calm estimates of how many Americans will be killed in the first surprise attack if Russia should push its buttons first. The number varies from 40 to 60 million casualties. We can actually, without hysteria, contemplate this, and apparently conceive with some measure of equanimity the retaliatory extinction of 40 million other lives.

But I suppose the ideas are so awesome that they do not really penetrate our minds. Neither, apparently, do the warnings of the experts that further development of such deadly mechanisms might even destroy the globe itself, or at least render it uninhabitable, for in the face of these warnings we continue the incredible race. Has Mother Earth herself become expendable?

It should be a shock to human reason to realize that the vast and intricate systems of offense and defense which are being set up by the great powers are more and more being designed to operate with "the minimum of human judgement." Just press a few buttons and the missiles will fly and the bombs roar. But you must press them instantly when the alarm comes; a few seconds' delay may bring annihilation to your country!

And who is to do the pressing? As the technical devices are elaborated and perfected it is likely that the alarm and the consequent button-pushing may all be brought about wholly by electronic gadgets and robots. Man will not have to make decisions or act. An ironic end to *Homo sapiens* if, as Colonel Harvey W. Shelton recently suggested, his extinction should be brought about by "a two-way, intercontinental exchange of ballistic missile forces that was triggered off by one radar which could not tell the difference between a meteorite and an ICBM." The ultimate perfection of automation: human judgment, the human mind, is to be made expendable!

Sometimes in black moments I wonder whether a strange suicidal urge, like that of the mysterious lemmings, has infected mankind, and is driving them on to global destruction. But I cannot believe it, for today there seems to be an even more widespread urge to life. Here in America the birth rate has risen amazingly. I look at the latest photograph of one of my many academic daughters and her family: Mary and John, and Jimmy aged seven, and Priscilla aged six, and Tommy four, and the twins Ellen and Henry, and the dog, large and protective—all healthy and cheerful, proudly loving one another and their home. Just a sample of a million American families, utterly aloof from thoughts of missiles and H-bomb fallout, the urge of life against the shadow of death. It is hard to think of them as expendable, or as future button-pushers.

What does the future hold for Mary and John and Jimmy and Priscilla and Tommy and the twins? Will the deadly spiral of expendability persist until it involves them all in the ultimate global catastrophe? Its causation by deliberate war we have a chance of avoiding; before human reason is completely expended we may reach some rational pact with possible foes. But sheer accident, the mistake of some stupid underling, the failure of a gadget, may push the button and produce the final holocaust, if we continue playing with these devastating devices.

What will the world be like after this up-to-date atomic-electronic Doomsday? Will there be anyone left to murmur Shakespeare's prophecy: "The cloud-capped towers, the gorgeous palaces,/The solemn temples, the great globe itself,/ Yea, all which it inherit, shall dissolve."

Perhaps even if we rich and highly mechanized nations expend ourselves out of existence, some of the "have-nots," too poor to throw themselves and their possessions on the dump heap, may survive the storm. They may preserve in their remote Shangri-La enough of the precious things of the past to start the few survivors of mankind on a new Renaissance, on a wiser, simpler way of life, cherishing the activities of the spirit and the beauty of art and nature, a life that does not lead to the spiral of expendability. And will they, I wonder, dig out and piece together and treasure the ruins of some of the buildings we would have carted off to the dump?

THE LOST HALF-CENTURY

⚹.⚹ Written in 1960 and published in the *Saturday Review* for May 14 of that year.

In future ages, when historians and lovers of literature brood over the past and try to sense the temper of bygone times, they will be able to read about and experience Athens in the fifth century B.C., Rome in the Augustan age, Europe in the Middle Ages, England in the eighteenth century, and many other eras, but one will be muted and dead—America in the first half of the twentieth century. Startling though it seems, this highly vocal age through which we have been living will in all probability have faded out of view. Why? Because nearly all books printed during this period are on paper that is expected to disintegrate within twenty to a hundred years.

A prominent specialist in the field of the preservation of documents, W. J. Barrow, recently wrote that "most library books printed in the first half of the twentieth century will be in an unusable condition in the next century."

Though few people have been conscious of this situation, and still fewer have been aware of its implications, librarians have been growing increasingly concerned about it ever since the introduction of ground wood and chemical wood fiber papers in the last decades of the nineteenth century. The custodians of great libraries have realized that they were "piling up mountains of paper only to watch these mountains disintegrate before their eyes," as a recent article on the subject expressed it.

Built-in obsolescence, as we have known for some time, has been the technique of many American manufacturers. The object is to force the customer to replace his purchase years before it would need to be replaced if it had been properly made. Even in the construction of our houses, we experience, to a very considerable extent, the trouble and expense of a planned, deliberate deterioration.

But must modern books also have obsolescence built in? For this has been done even more extensively and universally with books than with other manufactured items, though not, I believe, so consciously and deliberately. This fact is a body blow to every scholar and lover of books.

Microfilm, tape recordings, and other mechanical devices of recent years are methods by which we may possibly preserve the past and make it live again. On microfilm, especially, a great deal of work has been done, and there is reason to believe that film, properly processed and stored, may last for several centuries. But we cannot yet know. And though microfilm will obviously be of great value in preserving records, its use presents grave administrative and practical difficulties.

Can a scholar sit comfortably surrounded by them, dipping in here and there, as he is able to do when happily entrenched among piles of books? Can a poet carry a micro-film lovingly in his pocket and savor it as Keats did his little volumes of Shakespeare, which my friend the late Professor Caroline Spurgeon found in a private library in Princeton? They are seven small volumes of Shakespeare, printed in 1814, which John Keats had loved and read and carried about with him and annotated in the margins, and through which we can now feel close to the mind and hand of the tragic young poet. And what of the young poets of our own age? Will there be no shelter for the work of their minds, the poets who, like so many in the past, are not appreciated by their contemporaries, but whom readers of two or three hundred years from now might understand and love?

Let us not forget how, with the long years of Puritan intellectual dominance, the lyric poets, the Cavaliers, the Metaphysicals were thrust aside in the seventeenth century, almost forgotten. But in the sound little volumes of their age they waited, some for a couple of centuries, until "in God's good time" prowling readers picked their dusty books from the shelves, fame came again to the poet, and our literary heritage was enriched.

Not so with gifted poets of the 1900s, who may by sheer accident have failed to win much recognition. I know of one such book, an exquisite one. The first edition will soon melt into dust, the plates have been destroyed, no one can redis-cover it in the twenty-second century. It will never have a second chance. It is odd to realize that it will probably have as companions in oblivion most of the highly successful and acclaimed poems of the last fifty years!

Of course a few famous books and some essential records of the last half-century will survive or be continually reproduced. At least one newspaper, the *New York Times*, has been printing a few copies daily on rag paper (more recently it has used microfilms), and these will no doubt be usable for many years. For a long time it was thought that the use of rag paper would assure the survival of works of permanent value, though the cost would be practically prohibitive. But the experience of the Library of Congress has shown that this is by no means a certain and lasting device.

In a letter written to me on March 18, 1960, L. Quincy Mumford, Librarian of Congress, alludes to this discouraging experience. He speaks of the whole grave problem of the perishable quality of book paper as "one that has concerned librarians for some decades. With each passing year it has become more and more acute." But he is encouraged by the research now being done. Currently, he believes, the outlook is bright.

For a definite effort to grapple with this great problem of deteriorating paper has indeed been undertaken. In 1956 the Council on Library Resources was incorporated as an independent nonprofit body, with offices in Washington, D.C. It was established with a grant of five million dollars from the Ford Foundation to be expended over a five-year period "for the purpose of aiding in the solution of the problems of librarians generally and of research libraries in particular." The organization conducts its work chiefly through grants or contracts to appropriate organizations and individuals. Among the problems considered is, naturally, the matter of paper preservation. One study of this question has produced useful results and a second is well on the way. The outcome of this effort by highly competent experts will no doubt be the production of more lasting paper and binding for our future publications. The books of the second half of the twentieth century may largely survive. But the great bulk of newspapers, typescripts, periodicals, pamphlets, and books of the first half of the century is already crumbling away.

To whom, then, are we to leave the selection of some surviving material? Wholly to chance? Or should some authoritative body be set up to plan a comprehensive and wise collection? Possibly the Council of Learned Societies might be given the task. Or is the danger of censorship and bias inherent in any such authority worse than the peril of oblivion?

I notice in the laments of librarians great alarm at the "prohibitive cost" of some suggested expedients. They seem to feel, presumably from bitter experience, that the richest country in the world will not be willing to spend enough money to embody its great books in a form destined to last. I am not sure that this is the gravest obstacle. If a vast sum were made available for rescuing within the next fifty years representative writing and records of the recent past, are any of us really capable today of choosing what the future should know of the vanishing half-century?

Of recent years we have heard terrifying reports of the violation of the sanctity of libraries, of how a government can, by destroying certain books and records and altering texts and encyclopedias, expunge from history a man or an idea obnoxious to the party in power. Will this sort of thing happen now? The circumstances of the next few decades may make the crime of suppression and slanting by selective reproduction very tempting. Indeed, I hesitate to publicize the situation lest some of our ruthless propaganda organizations rush in to seize the opportunity.

Meditating on this strange condition to which man's scientific development and ingenuity have now brought us, I feel some envy of the ages of long ago. On a table in my modest home library rests a shabby, attractively fat little old book, an Erasmus Bible, printed in 1551. The pages are a bit yellowed but in excellent condition, the corners of the paper unbroken and firm. The small woodcuts are clear, the text perfectly legible. Four hundred years have left the volume intact.

There is also a set of the works of Martin Luther, twelve fat folios bound in vellum, printed in 1553–73 and long in the possession of a monastery whose monks annotated, queried, and criticized in the margins of the text. We are still able to read their opinions. Traveling further back in time, my mind arrives admiringly in medieval Europe, where I can see thousands of monks in hundreds of *scriptoria* devotedly copying, with lasting ink and on long-lived parchment, the great writings of the past, creating manuscripts which we, centuries later, can still read. The chain of culture, the continuity of thought, was not wholly broken.

Another picture comes to my mind, of that community

at Qumran by the Dead Sea 2,000 years ago, whose scrolls have recently been discovered and read with deepest interest. When another 2,000 years have passed, will any records or documents of our era exist, to give some image of our present America to the men of that far-off time—should any men still survive?

CALLING ALL WOMEN!

⚶⚶ Written in 1957 and published in the *Ladies Home Journal*'s June issue of that year, under the title "Wanted —Women to Help." My work in life had been concerned chiefly with scholarship and higher education and not with the special responsibilities of my sex in the fields with which most of this article deals. I had happened to be for many years in touch with the problems of nursing education and had known some of the most distinguished leaders of that profession, and I had of course been concerned with the supply of teachers. But only in the years of my retirement, in touch with some of the grave human problems caused by the changed social patterns of the time, did I become painfully aware of the failure of my sex to live up to its hereditary obligations. Then I wrote this essay.

ALL my life I have been concerned with the education of women and their place in our communities and our nation. The professions have been of special interest to me, and also the national service rendered by women in time of war. During World War II, I played a part in the organization of the Navy WAVES.

As I now observe the greatly changed and changing pattern of our American society, I am distressed to see that many of the duties and services traditionally performed by women are not being adequately carried on, so that much avoidable human suffering results, and considerable peril to the future of our country. In the changed social and economic structure of today, the old ways of meeting these ills do not avail. Some fundamental changes must be faced, some new order established.

The following informal dialogues present in concrete form examples of the facts that alarm me (the cases are drawn from real life) and a conceivably possible solution—or, if not now possible, at least a stimulus to some hard thinking and drastic effort.

"Poor old Captain Josiah Plant!" said the Skipper. "I hear his rheumatism is much worse. I'm worried about him and his wife," she added.

"Hasn't he a Coast Guard pension?" I asked.

"Yes, a tiny one, and it buys less and less each year. They're both over eighty. She's got a bad leg, can't walk; just pushes herself about a bit in a wheeled chair. They own their little house, but it's in that remote country township. They've no children, no relatives, and they're terribly proud.

"They nurse each other as well as they can, with occasional brief help from the district nurse, and most days one of them is able to cook up some food. But what's going to happen on days when neither one can get about?"

"They ought to have 'Meals on Wheels,' " said I.

"What?"

" 'Meals on Wheels.' Here, look at this picture. It's a plan carried out by the British Women's Voluntary Services. A small van brings hot meals to old people like your Plants, people who love their little homes and ought not to be shut into an institution, but who really can't take much physical care of themselves any more. There are a few such programs in this country—one in Philadelphia, I know; one planned for New York; best of all, the year or more of voluntary humane service of American Mennonite Youth.

"It would be cruel to separate the Plants or tear them from their house and their church. If we could send in a home helper to clean up a bit and give them some hot food occasionally, what a lot of human suffering we'd mitigate, and what a lot of pressure on hospitals and homes for the aged we'd relieve."

"Home helpers would sure be a blessing," said the Skipper, "to young mothers with new babies and a lot of other little children to care for and cook for. Do you remember young Mrs. Elijah Brown leaving the country hospital with her wee son four days after he was born, and those five other small children of hers in the old car who greeted her with shouts of joy?"

"Yes, her doctor was worried about her. He told me it was a real problem for women like that. They can't possibly afford to pay the hospital charges for more than three or four days and so they go home to families where there's often no one to help with the housework and no kindly neighbor at hand—as in Mrs. Brown's case. 'We tell them to be sure to take it easy at first,' said the doctor, 'but how can they?' "

"I'll bet," exclaimed the Skipper, "the dishes for the whole four days were waiting in the sink for Mrs. Brown's return. And as for the dirty clothes waiting! Your home helpers would be a godsend in such cases! Why shouldn't we have a countrywide corps of them, with Meals on Wheels, too, like these nice, kindly-looking W.V.S.'s in the picture?"

"The tendency in this country," I pointed out, "is to do things of this kind locally instead of nationally. Besides, you can't find enough women to travel from house to house and undertake such humble, drudging service, even when paid for it. Helen, who's been deep in social-welfare and public-health work for years, you know, tells me some of her organizations have had the same bright idea, but they can find hardly any women, almost nobody, to do this home helping."

"What can we do, then?"

"The mothers and the babies will struggle along somehow, I suppose, and we'll shut all the crippled and aged up in institutions, or put them out on the polar ice to freeze as some Eskimos are said to do—unless some miracle produces a supply of visiting angels."

"Where," asked the Skipper a few days later, "can I find some husky young persons with two hands and two feet and a kind heart? No special brains or training required, but the hands and feet indispensable, and particularly the kind heart."

"I've no idea," said I. "They all seem so busy. What do you want them for?"

"Three of them," she replied, "I'll send right over to Marian Laing's house. I had a talk with her yesterday."

"I haven't seen her for a long time. How's her spinal arthritis?"

"Worse, especially in this winter weather, so that she's badly crippled. And she's got other ailments too. But what's giving her sleepless nights and wearing her out with worry and perplexity is how to get her aged mother cared for. The old lady is ninety-four, you know. She fell and cracked a vertebra in her spine. Now the spine is better, but she's practically bedridden and has to have nursing attention twenty-four hours a day."

"Mercy! Can't Marian put her in the hospital?"

"She *was* in the hospital for six weeks. Then they said she must leave. Yes, really! They said hospitals couldn't keep old people for long stays; they needed their rooms for younger patients in emergencies, who could be cured and restored to active life."

"Heavens!" said I. "What's the condition of the old lady now?"

"Excellent organically, say the doctors. She may live five years or more! But some of her bodily functions don't work quite normally, and she needs to be lifted and turned at frequent intervals. She's an amiable, nice-mannered old lady, but gets confused and forgetful. She can't remember to push a buzzer, Marian says, just calls out loudly when she needs attention. It all adds up to round-the-clock nursing —somebody always at hand. The doctors say that will be absolutely necessary as long as she lives."

"Marian can't possibly lift her," said I. "Are there any other relatives?"

"No, absolutely none. Marian was able to get three nurses to care for the old lady while she was in the hospital—at a staggering cost. But when she had to leave, and Marian tried to arrange to care for her in her own home, there wasn't a nurse who would undertake to come for more than a few days—at *any* price."

"Does she have to have real trained nurses—R.N.'s, you know?"

"No, indeed. All she needs now is some simple mechanical attendance. Anybody with two hands and two feet and a kind heart could give it."

"Practical nurses, then?"

"They charge almost the same as the R.N.'s, and anyway, there aren't any available. This is a dreadful part of the country in which to get nurses, prosperous and populous though it is."

"What about a nursing home?"

"Same problem. None would take the old lady without special nurses, three a day. So the doctors say."

"What's the answer, then?"

"There's isn't any final one. But Marian had to send the old lady to Bevington, off in Massachusetts, where they have spent their summers and have friends, and where there *are* some kindly women who, at a price, will nurse the old lady."

"So it's settled, for the moment?"

"Except that the nursing—they don't live in—costs Marian

a thousand dollars a month and that's all the income she's got. She's using up her savings fast. And suppose that she herself cracks up and has to be hospitalized, as is quite likely."

"It's tragic," said I. "What's the good of keeping people alive to old age with our modern miracle drugs and treatments and then leaving them in a bleak world without care?"

"The trouble lies partly, I suppose," meditated the Skipper, "in the fact that we've never got the nursing profession properly organized. The great leaders of the past raised its standards higher and higher. And we're certainly devoutly thankful for the highly trained nurses when we're gravely ill. But they're too scarce and too expensive for ordinary middle-class people except in brief emergencies. So we've been trying the 'practical nurses,' but now they're scarce too and cost almost as much as the trained ones. Where do we go from here?"

"It's one of the grave shortages that afflict the nation," said I. "You hear complaints on every side—from hospitals, training schools, health services, suffering families with invalids young and old, difficult situations everywhere. There simply aren't enough nurses, trained or practical, enough nurses' aides except in a few hospitals, enough sturdy, kindly women, untrained but willing to lend a helping hand to the old and the crippled in time of need, at a wage the middle class can pay."

"And there won't be," concluded the Skipper, "unless some miracle produces a supply of visiting angels."

"Have you ever," asked the Skipper one winter evening, "watched a rather feeble teacher trying to handle forty husky boys and girls in an overcrowded classroom in a junior high school?"

"Happily, no," said I. "Have you?"

"Yes. Joan Elmont, you know, is on the board of education in her town, and took me to visit one of their schools. She's very concerned about the shortage and quality of teachers, and I don't wonder. Out in her state things are even worse than here. That poor young teacher I saw faced a class twice too big for her and she hadn't the brains or the force of personality to control them or to hold their interest. Some of the bigger boys were noisy and insolent. When she rapped and called 'Order, please,' they shouted 'Make mine beer'—copying Marlon Brando, you know. I longed to have a try at them."

"Did you get a chance to talk with her after the class?" I asked.

"Yes, and found her upset and depressed, on the verge of a nervous breakdown, I'm afraid. She's overworked, teaching one class right after another, with hundreds of papers to correct and clerical work to wade through after she escapes from the school; and a crippled, invalid sister to take care of when she gets home."

"Can't she get a practical nurse to look after her sister and give her a chance to rest?" said I.

"I asked her," answered the Skipper, "but she replied that she couldn't possibly afford a nurse. A teacher's salary, she protested, is only about the same as a nurse's nowadays."

37

"It's all very disturbing," I mused.

"More than disturbing," said the Skipper. "How are our children going to get really educated?"

"God knows," I answered. "Because poor as that teacher you saw was, ten years from now there won't be half as many teachers, even as good as she, in proportion to the vastly growing number of children we ought to educate."

"Unless," echoed the Skipper with a wry smile, "some miracle produces a supply of academic angels."

"Academic angels!" I protested. "Even they would be appalled by the statistics of the numbers they'll have to teach a few years from now, because of the soaring birth rate. Experts have figured that if we're to have even tolerably educated teachers for the children of a few years from now, then *half of all the graduates of all the colleges of the country will have to enter the teaching profession.* You and I both know that there's not the *faintest* chance of their doing that. There are too many other attractive fields of work, far, far more attractive to the great majority.

"So," I continued, "even if Congress appropriates many millions of dollars to help build more classrooms, as the President asks, classrooms will be of no use, without teachers in them."

"Besides that," added the Skipper to increase the gloom, "of the graduates who *do* go into teaching, with glorious exceptions, we rarely get the top people."

"The teachers' colleges," I objected, "say that situation is improving: that they're getting a better quality of candidate now; but, even so, the supply is far too meager. No,

38

whatever our efforts to make teaching a more lucrative and socially alluring profession, there's just no chance of our achieving even a moderately good teacher for every class-room. We'll always have a few born teachers who couldn't be hired to do anything else, but—"

"But *look!*" interrupted the Skipper. "What about this idea of teaching by television that some people are pushing? You know, *put* a great teacher in every classroom—on the television screen. Then, they say, one person can teach thousands and thousands. Of course that's not so."

"Not really," I agreed. "Still, there's something in it. It could help a lot—always provided that besides the great personality on the screen and the scenes and demonstrations shown there, you have real teachers, more like tutors, per-haps, to be in close human contact with the pupils, in small groups, to interpret to them, answer questions, oversee their work and activities—be sure that they *did* work and *were* active, not just an absorbing sponge, a passive audience. I'm perfectly sure that most children and young people need the warmth, the spark, the push they can get only from human contact with a real, live, present teacher. Abraham Lincoln didn't need it, but then there aren't many like him."

"That's a possible scheme," said the Skipper meditatively. "I can see it working in lots of places—helping and supple-menting the regular staff. And these 'tutors,' as you called them, wouldn't have to be very mature and experienced would they? With supervision, couldn't you manage with a lot of young assistants, keen young people, trained as apprentices?

"You remember the 'engineering aides' we trained during World War II, because of the dangerous shortage of engineers? Well, this is a time of dangerous shortage, too, one which threatens our country with masses of ill-educated citizens, and a feeble-minded electorate.

"A good many of the 'tutors' might get fascinated by the work—because of course there's nothing more fun than teaching, if you like it—and go on to become wise and experienced teachers." Her hopeful voice died down.

"No," I lamented. "It's no good. We couldn't possibly get enough young people to want to try being apprentice teachers—not enough to make a go of it on any considerable scale—not unless some miracle changed the minds of a lot of young Americans."

We fell into silence and gazed at the dying fire. We are both teachers, the Skipper and I, and sometimes we don't like the present look of our profession. It was late. The red embers paled to gray.

I was walking along the main street of a busy, tidy small city on a crisp, sunny morning. At the post office the Stars and Stripes flew as usual, as it did on another large, official-looking building next door, which bore the sign "Women's National Service Corps." Coming and going briskly through its swinging doors were young women in a uniform strange to me, horizon blue with collars and arm insignia of various colors—lemon yellow, dark blue, crimson, white—and smart caps with a silver eagle on the front.

Presently I found myself inside and entering a large

assembly hall, where hundreds of young women not in uniform were seated. They rose and stood politely when an efficient and friendly looking older woman, in the horizon-blue uniform, appeared on the speakers' platform. She smiled cheerfully, and invited them to be seated.

"Recruits of the Women's National Service Corps," she said, "I am the commandant of this fifteenth district. I welcome you to the service of your country, to those duties of humanity, healing and care, education and enlightenment, which have been for centuries the peculiar functions of women.

"You will all recall today the dramatic circumstances in which our corps was born, the tragic state of the world and the grave sufferings and dangers in our own country caused by the extreme shortages of workers in these humanitarian fields. So serious was the situation that the new President of the United States declared a state of emergency and called upon the women of the nation to rally to its aid.

"The great organizations of women, the women of the churches, the schools, industry, rose in reply. They formed a council to speak for them and the council sent to the President that message which has become historic:

" '*We, the women of the United States of America, claim equal right with our brothers to serve our country. As we share equal rights of citizenship, we ask to share in return equal duties. As our brothers are drafted for military service, we ask that we be drafted for services which are tradition-ally and naturally the peculiar duty of women—the care of human beings in adversity and bitter need, the beneficent work of nursing, and the teaching and guidance of the youth of the nation.'*

"This moving appeal from the women was granted, and so this corps of ours was born. In it you now have the proud privilege of serving.

"You will receive here some basic instruction and will be consulted and tested to determine where you should be placed in the three great divisions in which our work is classified: nursing, home helping, teaching. Then you will each be given some special preliminary training in the work of the division where you belong, before you pass on to your apprenticeship in one of these great fields of useful and satisfying service.

"May you be happy in it and do credit to our corps, and may your experience in these years of national service make you stronger and more understanding during all the rest of your life!"

I awoke reluctantly, warmed with pride.

"You've been nodding," said the Skipper.

"Yes, I slept a bit and I had a dream—that was not quite all a dream." I described it.

"Goofy!" exclaimed the Skipper. "Draft American women! I can't imagine anything less likely to happen!"

"Yes," I agreed. "It couldn't happen. Only a miracle could make it happen; and we don't go in for miracles these days. But then, *what are the women of America going to do to meet these crying needs of their people?*"

THE NATURE OF WOMAN

🌿🌿 Written in 1958. The material about these three Cape Cod women is drawn almost entirely, and in large part quoted literally, by permission, from that rich store of Cape history and legend *The Narrow Land: Folk Chronicles of Old Cape Cod*, by Elizabeth Reynard.

MIDNIGHT on old Cape Cod, no moon; Cynthia Gross leaned forward in the saddle and touched with her warm, capable hand her little mare's neck. The horse knew the way in the darkness and Cynthia gave her rein. The young rider, despite enormous vitality and a calm sense of power, was weary in body and soul. Forcing her horse at breakneck pace, she had ridden fifteen miles that day, to reach a woman believed to be dying in childbirth. She had fought to save mother and child, working with the knowledge and daring that made her the best loved midwife and doctor that the Cape has ever known.

Passing by night over treacherous bog-trails, through "Indian Forests," along desolate moors, she frequently had cause for gratitude that her father had taught her the Indian tongue. But, before she had practiced midwifery for many years, so widely was her skill heralded that those who had no personal knowledge of her, recognized the indomitable little horsewoman with her midwife's bundle strapped at the rear of the saddle and her crisp bonnet mounted high on her smoothly coifed head. Every man and woman on the Cape, one might almost say every living creature, wished Cynthia Gross Godspeed. Her ability to alleviate human suffering was almost equaled by her proficiency with injured animals and birds. A broken-winged crow, a lame hen, a blind dog waited at her doorstone; and once in the night her little niece, Miriam, sleeping soundly in the feather poster, was ordered to "lie over" while Aunt Cynthia placed in the "cozy-hole" a tiny, shivering lamb.

Almost a fetish became the belief in her medical prowess; almost a fable the story of her midwifery; five hundred babies brought out of the womb, often in homes of poverty without convenience or resource; and by her capable, cool ministrations, never a mother lost.

As she rode toward home that night, her level eyes peered into the blackness of the highroad. She had won a sharp battle with death, but she ached in every bone.

Wellfleet Methodist Church loomed against the sky. Past the Meeting House the mare would turn into the shortcut through the cemetery, then over the hill to Gull Pond, to the farmhouse where Cynthia and her nine sisters lived; all ten of them clear-minded, energetic women, skilled singers and musicians.

Tired as she was, Cynthia remembered her Sunday bonnet with its butterfly bow. After the last Sabbath Meeting, when she discovered how the rain was falling, she had hesitated, blushed a little, turned back into the church and deposited her best bonnet in her pew. Bareheaded she had walked home in the mild summer rain, through the Burying Acre, over the hill, past Gull Pond, from whose dark blue waters the Gross sisters were said to have stolen the color of their eyes.

Cynthia decided to retrieve her Sabbath cap before its crisp allurement proved an irresistible temptation to some weak-willed church visitor. In the darkness of clouded midnight, Cynthia dismounted, found the Meeting House door open, and felt her way within.

The mare whinnied nervously; but to the young rider, whose life centered in the life of Cape Methodism, every inch of wall and flooring was familiar. Toward the front of the church she groped, slowly counting pews. Entering the "fourth from the front" she saw a white substance against the bare bench. That would be her Sunday bonnet. Reaching down to "pluck it up" she touched a dead man's face.

"Alas, poor soul," sighed Cynthia Gross, and she felt of the cold features again, to be quite sure that nothing was left to save.

"This must not be our pew," thought she. "I have miscounted in the dark."

So Cynthia entered the next pew and again saw a blurred whiteness, again reached down to it and touched a dead man's face.

Confusing to the mind at midnight! But Cynthia did not think it so. Instead she thought it was sad to be "laid out" without a burying box or a shroud. She surmised that the dead were drowned sailors from some wreck offshore.

45

"God rest their souls, where is my bonnet?" queried Cynthia anxiously, then perceived a nodding whiteness suspended from the aisle-post. Carefully, not to hurt the bow, Cynthia carried her bonnet outside, folded her night ridingcap and thrust it into her saddle pocket, donned her precious Sabbath headgear, mounted her mare, and rode homeward through night's shadowy trail.

Cynthia Gross is a refreshing acquaintance, I find, after a surfeit of the present-day American woman as she appears in books, press, television, and other forms of public expression. Different ages have, of course, startlingly different conceptions of the nature of women. Our current era (I write in the American scene of 1958) in spite of lip service to the equality of woman with man in education and careers, appears to be concerned chiefly with woman from the standpoint of sex, sometimes glamorizing, sometimes degrading it. Indeed, the American mind, as manifested in print and on the screen, often seems to wallow in an obsession with physical sex. So Evangelist Billy Graham has recently been pointing out with considerable vehemence.

The American woman herself—surely with millions of exceptions not apparent to the public view—appears to fall in happily with this conception of her role as a creature conscious constantly of her sex appeal. Note that the emphasis in television commercials dealing with products the advertisers want women to buy is most often on their efficacy in luring the male to physical contact.

Satiated with this overemphasis on sex, I have been enjoying a change by renewing acquaintance with some women

46

of our past. As I am living in a household on the outer shore of Cape Cod, with a tempting store of Cape history and legend, I have been thinking especially of a few contrasting figures from this distillation of the spirit and flavor of early America.

From Cynthia Gross I turn to Jane Bumpus. And she leads me to a quaint and little known institution of old New England—the "Widdow's Vandue." In the early days of the colonies there were no poorhouses. When a goodman died and left a widow with no money and no son to support her, the Selectmen put her up at auction, to sell her services for the next year to the highest bidder. She got a roof over her head and food to eat, and the town got payment for her work, money which helped pay for care of the aged who were entirely bedridden. Prices varied from over £10 for a young, comely widow to as low as ninepence for an elderly, feeble one, averaging in 1770 £3 per head. Fortunately the old women tended to die soon, but while they survived they were indeed a vexation to the town fathers, who had to provide clothes, burial, and medical care. Or were they *not* responsible for doctoring and drugs? When a widow exhausted in one year the amount allotted for medical care and was still ill, she had to go on without doctoring, unless her physician had a generous heart.

It sounds like a cruel system, but perhaps it was not so vicious in practice. After all, wives were scarce and useful, and most widows could soon marry again. At least the unwanted elderly females were not herded together as they often are today in overcrowded, underfinanced masses,

47

dominated by the senile and the aggressive. They were given while they could do it a useful job of work, and they lived in family units.

Occasionally a case vexed and puzzled the Selectmen for years at a stretch. Such was Jane Bumpus, widow of Louis Bumpus, direct descendant of the Sieur Louis Bompasse who came from France to the French colony in Canada and later migrated southward. When her "furrin" husband died, Jane was placed at "vandue."

Instead of a demure, downcast countenance, or a winning, eager smile, Jane faced the meeting squarely, scowled and cried "For shame," until reproved by the minister. A farmer in need of a "female hand" thought her worth taming. She was "bid in" and carted away to serve her "Widdow's yeare."

But Jane was of tough fibre. With no intention of perishing, she took no interest in her success at "vandue." Regularly, every year, she changed homes, falling always to lower estate. Yet she never suffered for clothes. What she needed to keep herself "decent" she appropriated; and if a family protested, she invited them to seek recompense from the Deacons and Selectmen, whom she called her "cruel stepfathers."

The Selectmen grew to hate her, for she understood how to blackmail them. If she detected a Deacon breaking the Sabbath by work on his woodpile, or an Elder wandering home from the tavern on Lecture Night, she called on the Elder or Deacon and suggested that a vote in the approaching town meeting to allow her some small spending-pence might bring her to feel that she had mistaken a truly charitable man for a Sabbath offender. Otherwise, she deemed it necessary to rise and publicly declare in Meeting that she was witness to an offense.

In this manner a large number of generous impulses developed among Deacons. The records include many charitable proposals in behalf of Mistress Bumpus. Unfortunately the bulk of them were "passed in the negativ."

Capable, ingenious, unfailingly devoted to children, Jane exerted herself when she pleased. If smallpox or diphtheria or black fever visited the youth of the community, she frequently dismissed herself from a service to which she was contracted and went to nurse a suffering child until the crisis was past. She put small value on her own existence. The children whom she nursed through illness became unswervingly devoted to her. They had seen Aunt Jane with her sharp tongue gentle, her keen eyes quiet, as she battled death.

When she died, the spite of the men who had held small, guilty hates in their hearts was reflected in the final consideration of "Jane Bumpus, deceased." The Widow Lovell had had eight shillings to "rig her for eternity"; Jane was given no winding sheet, only ninepence for a clean shift. A grave was dug in Poverty Corner, at the briary end of the Burying Acre; and as no notice of her funeral was posted, the minister came alone to the church to read over her body the service of the dead.

To his horror and bewilderment and the consternation of the grave-digger, when they two approached to nail her pine box preparatory to burial, it was discovered to be empty. Investigation revealed that four of the children she had nursed, all boys under sixteen, had carved a fine coffin into which they had laid her tenderly. Then the four of them bore her away to a place in the woods where they buried her, with such prayers as they knew. They planted the sod over her with fresh green pines and flowers, and erected a cross carved with the words:

Mistress Jane Bumpus
Wife of Sir Bumpus of France.

My third example of the nature of woman I cannot introduce by name. This scarlet-cloaked figure on a great black horse flashes through many versions of Cape legend. The Atwoods say she was Desire Atwood; the Paines say she was Bethia Paine; the Nickersons say she was Rose Nickerson; in fact there is no old Cape family to this day who does not claim to be related to that gallant rider. I can, however, name the ship she succored and the details of its troubled story can be verified from maritime records.

The ketch *Elinor*, homeward bound to Boston from the island of Nevis, laden with sugar and indigo, anchored in Nantasket Roads in November, 1689. In her cabin lay a woman, four men, and a boy, ill with the dreaded smallpox. The ship was short of provisions and medicines, and the wind failed. So the Captain, with the mate and a sailor, set out in the ship's boat for Boston to get aid.

Left on board in charge was one seaman, James Thomas, with only a young boy to help him tend the whole ship and care for the six sufferers. Then new disaster struck. The *Elinor* was boarded by pirates, who knocked Thomas senseless and locked him and the boy in the cabin with the smallpox patients, then headed the ship out to sea. But the pirates were no more fortunate than the Captain had been. They failed to get supplies at Provincetown and so sailed for Barnstable. Soon they ran aground. Despairing of floating the ship they abandoned her and disappeared in the pine woods on shore.

So there was James Thomas, conscious again now, with his boy helper and six smallpox patients locked in a dark, foodless cabin stenching with a foul plague. But he had his seaman's knife and as soon as all was quiet on the ketch, he hacked his way out of the boarded-up cabin. Before the tide rose he plunged into the water and swimming between bars and wading across them, he made his way to the beach and found a roadway, along which he wearily trudged. But soon there appeared, cantering down the road on a great black horse, a woman with a scarlet cloak flying at her shoulder. She drew up when she saw James Thomas, wet, haggard, well nigh frozen in the keen November air. He told her the story of the ketch *Elinor*, and of the six souls dying in the cabin, with poor water, no food, no medicines to save them.

The scarlet-cloaked lady took out her purse and thrust money on James Thomas, and explained to him carefully and clearly how to reach the house of Mr. Samuel Treat, minister, nurse, doctor, who was never afraid to face disease and who would come, bringing the needed supplies, as soon as he was summoned. Then, without further comment, she wheeled her horse and made for the shore. While Thomas stared after her in wonder, she rode that horse through the November water, over the first bar, swimming him expertly through the deep eddies; over the second bar, again through deep water, until he reached the side of the *Elinor*. There she climbed the Jacob's ladder to the deck, while the horse plunged, whinnied, then turned at her order and slowly swam to the shore.

When James Thomas brought Samuel Treat, in a shallop, some four hours later, the two men found the cabin clean and sweet; the cook's galley washed; a warm fire glowing; a pot on the stove; disease-racked bodies washed; broken sores bandaged; fever cooled by "applicashuns." A woman's voice was singing; and in the cabin there was comfort and hope, and occasionally a little laughter. On deck in the rigging, the ketch *Elinor* flew the strangest signals that ever a ship displayed: one scarlet cloak, drying, one gray woven dress, two homespun hose with scarlet bands ringed around the top of them, and six loom-linen petticoats. The rescuers were met by a laughing figure in seaman's jacket and trousers, with a soap-sponge in one hand and a ship's pail in the other.

The Atwoods say she was Desire Atwood; the Paines say she was Bethia Paine; the Nickersons say she was Rose Nickerson. No wonder that every old Cape family claims close relationship to the girl who rode her black horse over two bars and three deeps to the rescue of the ketch *Elinor*.

I like my three examples of the nature of woman. The

resemblances between them are obvious. Are their qualities typical of many of the sex today? Perhaps not so often in the complex society of the present as they were in colonial and frontier days. Or perhaps they are merely obscured by the outward fashion of our time?

The social historian of the future, studying the remains of our novels, our films, the advertisements of books and movies, will doubtless record our women as animated almost wholly by preoccupation with sex. Whereas in fact the vast majority of American women today are by force of circumstances compelled to labor more continuously, in and out of the home, than any women of the past in a society with a comparable standard of living. Indeed, there has never been a nation, I strongly suspect, of more useful and hard-working women, or one whose women have been less realistically portrayed in an age of so-called realism.

Written in May, 1954, for a radio script which was part of a project carried out by Broadcast Music, Incorporated, and the Society of American Historians. This collection of a hundred scripts on episodes in our history, written by as many American historians, was entitled "The American Story." It was distributed without charge to radio stations throughout the country and was widely used. In 1956 *The American Story* was published in book form by the Channel Press, New York, and was chosen by two book clubs for distribution. So my little script has traveled far. The invitation from the Society of American Historians to write the section on "The San Francisco Conference and the United Nations," those great events in which I was privileged to play a small part, gratified me deeply. It would have pleased, I thought, my very distinguished teacher, James Harvey Robinson, under whom I had taken a master's degree in Medieval History fifty-four years before.

THE San Francisco Conference which gave birth to the Charter of the United Nations grew out of a bitter need felt by men and women everywhere in our broken world. World War II was then raging—the most terrible of all wars. As its horrors sank into the minds and hearts of

Americans, they began to wish with an increasingly desperate eagerness that something could be done to prevent such horrors in the future. The world, they now sensed, had become a small place, the interests and the emotions of the various nations entangled with one another. Obviously, it was no longer possible for America to wrap its oceans about itself, withdraw from international affairs, and retreat to comfortable isolation.

The great national organizations that had felt intense interest in the League of Nations and hoped for our country's membership in it now began again to demand some world organization for peace and security. They found a ready response in the hearts of parents whose sons were facing death on the battlefields and on the oceans. The cry of our people for some stupendous effort to stop future wars rose in a mighty crescendo. By the time the United States delegation went to San Francisco in April, 1945, for the conference that was to create a definite Charter of the United Nations, we felt carried forward on a great wave of support and of prayers from our fellow countrymen.

President Franklin Roosevelt and his advisers planned with considerable astuteness to avoid at least some of the difficulties which had wrecked the possibility of United States membership in the League of Nations. He wanted to keep the new project out of and above party politics; and he wanted to make the people of the country at large feel that their ideas and wishes were being consulted and followed. His success in raising the issue above party politics was largely due to the personality and influence of that remarkable man, Senator Arthur Vandenberg. A stanch Republican, very influential in his party, Vandenberg had been an isolationist. He had, however, come to see clearly that it was impossible for our country to stand aloof from world affairs, and that we must now lead some cooperative effort for peace and security among all nations.

The delegation which represented our country at San Francisco was constructed on a bipartisan basis. Besides its leader, Secretary of State Stettinius, it included the Democratic Chairman, Senator Connally; and the Republican Minority Leader, Senator Vandenberg, of the Senate Committee on Foreign Relations; the Democratic Chairman, Congressman Bloom; and the Republican Minority Leader, Dr. Eaton, of the House Committee on Foreign Affairs; and two members at large: Commander Harold Stassen of the United States Navy, formerly governor of Minnesota, a Republican, and the one woman member, a Democrat, Dean Virginia C. Gildersleeve of Barnard College, Columbia University. This setup of the committee was successful in keeping the Charter free from party politics.

To make the people at large feel that they had some hand in this vital work, many national organizations were invited to send representatives to San Francisco to serve as "consultants," to hear reports of the progress of the Charter discussions and to make suggestions. Thus the whole population of the country had a chance to feel close connection with what we, their representatives and spokesmen, were doing in building a new world organization to keep the peace. All this contributed to producing general approval of the

Charter and its almost unanimous ratification by the Senate of the United States.

The other forty-seven nations whose representatives assembled at San Francisco seemed as eager as we were to stop future wars. Many of them had suffered far more terribly than we had during the war still raging. The four great powers which "sponsored" the conference—China, the United Kingdom, the United States, and the Union of Soviet Socialist Republics—had already prepared a draft of a Charter to serve as a basis of discussion.

At San Francisco, we agreed without much difficulty that our general purpose was to maintain international peace and security, to develop friendly relations among nations, and to promote human welfare and respect for human rights and fundamental freedoms for all without distinction as to race, sex, language, or religion. And we agreed that nothing in the Charter should authorize the United Nations to intervene in matters essentially within the domestic jurisdiction of any state.

In order to achieve our purposes, we had to set up some definite machinery. To reconcile disputes between countries and stop wars the machinery had to have, as we expressed it, "some teeth in it." The Security Council, as we designed it, had this. It is the only organ of the United Nations that has authority to enforce its decisions. It consists of the five great powers (France had been added to the original four), and six other nations elected from time to time by the General Assembly.

It is required to try in every possible way to bring about

peaceful settlements of disputes that arise and that may lead to war. But, if these efforts fail, the Security Council has, according to the Charter, armed forces provided by the different nations, and immediately available national air force contingents for combined international enforcement action. However, these weapons of enforcement never came into being as planned. The great powers could never agree in the Military Staff Committee on the setup of these armed forces. An army to act for the United Nations in stopping aggression in Korea was improvised, but the Security Council, for the greater part of these years, has had to function without any "teeth," without weapons to enforce its decisions.

This vital, central organ of the United Nations has been handicapped also by the veto power possessed by each of the Big Five, which, as used by Russia, has seemed a hindrance and a curse. People ask: Why did we ever adopt it at San Francisco? There were really two reasons. First, it seemed no decision could ever be carried out unless the five great powers were in unanimous agreement. Since this was so, why not recognize it by giving each a veto? The second reason was a practical one. Russia and the United States both insisted on having a veto. Our delegation was told that there was no chance of our getting the United States Senate to ratify the Charter unless the United States had a veto.

The smaller nations under the leadership of Australia fought long and violently against the veto. They accepted it finally because without it they could not have had a Charter, and they preferred some world organization, even with the veto, to a complete failure of the Conference.

Publicity about the United Nations has been so centered on the conflicts in the Security Council, and the headlines which people see have so vividly portrayed the political disputes and deadlocks there, that we have tended to overlook the really great constructive work for human welfare carried on by the United Nations. This concern for the well-being of humanity, for a good life for every man, woman, and child everywhere, is what is sometimes called "the soul of the Charter." It centers in the Economic and Social Council.

This Council consists of eighteen nations elected by the General Assembly of the United Nations. It works largely through commissions concerned with economic affairs in different parts of the world, social affairs, and human rights; and also through a large number of specialized agencies or affiliated organizations concerned with such vital matters as food and agriculture, the health of the world, banking and finance, educational and cultural relations, labor conditions, and the very terrible problem of refugees. If you could regularly read the *United Nations Bulletin*, and get a picture of the wonderful work for human welfare which is being done through this multitude of agencies, your hopes for the future would become brighter. In it you would learn, for example, about the joint effort of the World Health Organization and the Food and Agriculture Organization to remedy the tragic deficiency in the diets of millions of children in

59

various countries. Milk is what they acutely need. How to produce more milk under the agricultural conditions in the different lands the W.H.O. and the F.A.O. are effectively teaching; and in the places where milk cannot be produced, what substitutes are best, and how they can be obtained.

The Economic and Social Council is the center for all these activities, guiding and coordinating them. It has no authority whatsoever to enforce any of its decisions on the nations belonging to the organization. It can only recommend. It is like the community welfare councils with which we are familiar in a thousand towns in our country. They too have no power to enforce decisions, but when the various groups that come together realize that the plans will work for their good, they agree voluntarily. So it is with countries.

The General Assembly, sometimes called "The Town Meeting of the World," is the organ where each member nation—now seventy-six in all—has one vote. All problems and plans can be aired and discussed here. The General Assembly, however, is not, like Congress or Parliament, a legislative body with power to enforce its decisions. It has some power over the Trusteeship Council and the administration of countries under this guidance, and it does elect members of the Security and Economic and Social Councils. Otherwise it can only make recommendations. Most people do not realize this. They think a decision of the General Assembly has all the authority and force of the United Nations behind it. This feeling has caused some grave misunderstandings.

Because of the failure of the Security Council to function satisfactorily, our country has tended to throw more and more emphasis on the General Assembly and get it to act on critical questions. But if the General Assembly is ever to become that body of fundamental authority and power which some people wish, it will have to be drastically reorganized so that the Republics of Costa Rica and Liberia will not have as much voting strength as the Soviet Union and the United States of America. How would votes be allotted? If it is to be merely by population numbers, should we be willing to have India, for example, cast two or three times as many votes as the United States?

One very great difficulty is, of course, the possession of the veto power by the five great powers. Must that continue, and how? When at San Francisco we chose China, France, Britain, Russia, and the United States as the five great powers, how could we tell how long this would last? Who are the five great powers today? Who will they be a hundred years from now?

In the present state of our globe, where the nations live elbow to elbow, it is obvious that there will have to be some sort of world order. Perhaps it will all be under the domination of one great power. Let us devoutly hope not. But if this fate is not to befall us, we must have some general organization of nations, with each retaining its own individuality and control over its internal affairs. Should our present United Nations fail and be discontinued, as some isolationists now hope it may be, then we should just have to start all over again and build up painfully a new world organization. It seems infinitely better for us to fix our minds upon the many good things that our United Nations is now doing, build upon them, and try to remedy, as the years go on, the shortcomings that inevitably develop in a human machine faced with such an intricate and delicate task.

THE WHITE SACHEM OF

MASHPEE

⚜⚜ Written in 1955 as a script for the continuation of that project on "The American Story" carried on by Broadcast Music, Incorporated, and the Society of American Historians described in the prefatory note to "New Hope at San Francisco." They decided to make this second year's collection brief biographical sketches of Americans, well known or relatively obscure, who had played significant parts in our history.

The invitation to participate in this continuation reached me, as did a similar request the following year, while I was in my summer home on Cape Cod, that flavorful and intensely American peninsula from which and from nearby Plymouth so much of our national history and character originally sprang. As plenty of Cape material was at hand, I naturally chose a Cape figure. He was little known but picturesque and of real importance in the infancy of our nation—Richard Bourne. He came to the Massachusetts Bay Colony about the same time as did my ancestor Richard Gildersleeve. Perhaps Bourne came in the same ship, the small bark *James* which brought over Gildersleeve and about 100 other settlers in 1635. I know from the early records that my Richard was a "contumacious" person, and I conjecture that this other Richard had a touch of the same quality, along with his warm humanity, generosity, and vision.

RICHARD BOURNE, preacher-apostle to the Indians, the White Sachem of Mashpee on Cape Cod—few Americans have ever heard of him, yet to him we may owe in no small measure the nature of our great country as it exists today. We are English-speaking, lovers of freedom, our laws and our government derived in good part from ideas brought to the American wilderness by a few humble men and women who clung precariously to the edge of a savage continent: one hundred and two Pilgrims; half of them dead the first winter. Yet the Compact they signed on the *Mayflower* contains the kernel of our American form of government. And the village of Plymouth they set up was an *American* village, with town meetings, Thanksgivings, and in time white-steepled churches.

Richard Bourne was a thickset, vigorous man with a quick smile and a clear brain. He arrived in the early days of the colony, a young man with some money of his own and influence in England. Trained as a lawyer at the Inns of Court in London, his legal training was at once in demand. New colonists were arriving. Many deeds had to be drawn up for the purchase of land from the Indians. To do this, he realized that he must learn the language of the Wampanoag Indians. This he did promptly and well.

So, too, did certain of the ministers. They had come to America with missionary zeal, anxious to save the souls of the heathens who were thought to be the spawn of Lucifer, or the descendants of Cain. The poor puzzled Indians listening to brimstone sermons found them hard to take, whereas the good lawyer who refused to let them be cheated of their lands, who clearly believed in justice for Red Men as well as White Men, seemed to them an interpreter they could trust. Eager to get some grasp of the new civilization that confronted them, Indian leaders asked Richard Bourne to expound not only the White Man's laws but the White Man's religion. Hard put to it to make the Pilgrim faith understandable, Richard sought parallels in Indian tradition, and found in their stories of Gods and miracles and heroes similarity to some of the famous Biblical tales, like Noah and the Flood, and Jonah and the Whale. Skillfully he adapted Indian stories into their Christian counterparts. From these resemblances he built up a curious Indian faith, not altogether Christian, yet certainly not heathen.

Now many of the Praying Indians, as such converts were called, were hangers-on at the outskirts of the White Men's villages. Not so Richard Bourne's Praying Braves. He had purchased a large tract of salt meadows and forests at the shoulder of the great arm of land, called Cape Cod, that reaches into the sea south of Plymouth. This land he shared with his Indian converts and as more and more Indians sold or traded the sites of their villages, Richard realized that a time would come when natives who thought a bead or a kettle more valuable than many acres would be without hunting lands and homes. He appealed to the General Court for new grants until his lands extended in a belt completely across the entrance to the long peninsula of

Cape Cod. Then he petitioned the Court to set aside a grant adjoining his own, for the permanent use of Christian Indians. Incredulous outcry greeted this idea. It was a *madness*, men said, to encourage Indians to group together. Besides, the lands that this White Sachem wanted for his Redskins was agricultural land suitable for new settlers. Quietly, forcefully, Richard pleaded his case before the Court. The goodmen shook their heads in bewilderment, but they granted him a partial victory. Sixteen square miles of territory was set aside to belong, as the old deed puts it, "to the South Sea Indians and their children forever."

There was feasting and dancing when Richard rode back to Bourneland. That night a hundred pine torches were struck into the ground forming a fiery circle. Inside that circle the Indians began to build their own church. Richard taught them Christian doctrine and reading and writing. Now he taught them how to build with tools.

Gradually his army of Praying Braves grew in number. It was said to be between five and ten thousand skilled bowmen and spearmen, ready to die for their "little father" the White Sachem. Richard also acquired a reputation for magic. Squaws brought their babies to him for healing, so he sent to England for medical books and prescribed cures. In 1649 famine desolated the country. Richard fed his Praying Braves and their families with corn purchased at his own expense. Legal adviser, judge, teacher, doctor, nurse, architect, in later life he also became an ordained minister.

He had preached for some years to his fellow colonists in the little village of Sandwich, standing humbly, as became a "secular," on the stair below the top step of the pulpit. At first the goodmen eyed him askance, doubting, half-hostile. In time they became his loyal supporters and friends.

The powerful preacher-rulers of the Massachusetts Bay and Plymouth Colonies disputed among themselves about his ordination. "Better regularize this strange man's position" was apparently the consensus of opinion. "Many Christian souls are in his charge. As a minister of God he will no longer be able to partake in heathen practices."

John Cotton and John Eliot journeyed to the Kingdom of Mashpee to ordain Richard Bourne. In fact, to the ordination came all of the leading men of the colony including Governor Prince. Richard's people assembled on a wide unwooded hillside. Rank upon rank of armed Braves stood at attention, spears held ready to defend their White Sachem. Englishmen stared uneasily, curiosity tinged with fear. The host of impassive dark faces seemed to John Cotton and John Eliot "such an multitude as would make a swaying sea." And neither White Men nor Red Men seemed to realize that Richard Bourne held the key to understanding between the two opposing races who shortly would join in a battle to the death.

Less than five years after Richard's ordination Indian tocsins sounded their call for all-out war against the white invaders. King Philip's War it was called, you remember, a fight to the finish between colonists and redskins, one or the other to survive and rule. Indian runners carried to all Wampanoags and their allied tribes a summons to join Philip in his stronghold some miles west of Bourneland

67

where the final battles would be joined. Bonfires flared. Warpaint gleamed. There were freshly sharpened spears, newly feathered arrows, and stolen firewater and guns. Then down the length of the Cape came a disorganized horde of savages planning to attack the hard-pressed Puritan forces from the rear. To do this it was necessary for them to cross through the Mashpee Kingdom or the lands of Richard Bourne. They had expected to gather well-armed recruits from the Praying Braves of Mashpee. It never occurred to them that they might not be given safe conduct through Indian territory. Instead they found their way blocked, across the entire Cape, by well-ordered companies of trained spearmen and bowmen, while expert sharpshooters were hidden in the trees. The scrap-happy yelling bands launched a few feel-out skirmishes, then realized that to reach the army of the colonists they must first fight their way through Richard's Praying Braves. Group by group, turning, they straggled back to their homes.

Almost all military strategists agree that had King Philip won over even a small number of Richard's Praying Braves, or had these permitted the Cape Indians to pass through their territory, and attack the colonists from the east while they were battling Philip from the west, the Puritan forces would have been disastrously defeated. Horror and massacre would have followed. For a long time there would have been little heart for renewed colonization in that area. And we should not have been quite the same Americans that we are. Perhaps neither better nor worse but *certainly* different. Dutchmen or Frenchmen or the colonies of the South might have dominated our early traditions, have set the pattern of our ways.

In the thankfulness of a victory in which every white man capable of carrying a gun had done his utmost, the colonists made no special hero of Richard Bourne. After all, Richard had donned no sword. He had stayed at home and never struck a blow. Not long afterwards he disappeared. No one knows how he died or where his bones lie buried. The Mashpee Indians claimed that he had been murdered by a band of embittered warriors of Philip. Tradition says that his Praying Braves found his mutilated body and buried it secretly in the floor under the altar of their church. And now even the memory of the White Sachem of Mashpee lies buried in dusty archives. Yet seldom have Americans owed so much to the wisdom of one man.

⚓⚓ Written in 1956 for the continuation of the biographical broadcasts in "The American Story," as described in the prefatory note to "The White Sachem of Mashpee." In the goodly store of Cape material found in Henry C. Kittredge's *Shipmasters of Cape Cod* I was attracted by the dashing figure of Captain Elijah Cobb. So I went on to read his own autobiography, with its delightful mixture of naïvete, boldness, and sharp bargaining. It seemed to me amusing that just as our republic was being born there sprang to life, full fledged, the typical Yankee trader— Elijah Cobb and many another.

ELIJAH COBB was a lad from Cape Cod on the Massachusetts coast, who became master of a ship and traded with France at the time of her great Revolution and even dealt in person with the terrorist Robespierre.

He was typical of those enterprising and shrewd sailors who built up American shipping along the New England coast during the first years of our republic and developed international trade. Long before the swift and beautiful clipperships winged their way around the Horn, less famous vessels more humbly but boldly and cleverly brought renown to Yankee sails and Yankee traders. Thus they helped put our infant nation, weak and poor, on the first stages of the road—so long but so swiftly traveled—to the wealth and power we wield today.

As Captain Elijah Cobb wrote down his life story, we can follow it in his own words. His father died at sea, leaving a penniless widow and six children. Elijah went to work away from home at the age of six. (It was about the time of our Declaration of Independence.) When he was thirteen we see him seeking a job at the Boston docks, asking a strange captain for a job as cabin boy. "Can you cook?" says the captain. "Not much, but I can soon learn," says Elijah. So off he goes to Surinam (Dutch Guiana). There, with money acquired by gifts from the officers, he buys a barrel of molasses and some boxes of fruit. These he sells at a profit back in Boston, and gives his mother twenty dollars out of his twenty-one dollars of wages. Sailors were allowed these small, private ventures in our early days, many a successful trader started his mercantile career as cabin boy or common seaman when he bought out of his savings a barrel of molasses or a barrel of rum and brought it home to trade.

Cheered by his good start, Elijah became a sailor and coastal trader. He rose to be mate and later captain. At the age of twenty-four he married and soon sailed for Cadiz, Master of the Brig *Jane*, with a cargo of flour and rice.

The Reign of Terror was at its height in France, but Cobb was not worrying about terrorists; he was fearful of Algerian pirates cruising outside the Straits of Gibraltar. Then, to his surprise, he was picked up off Brest by a

French frigate and ordered into port. "And here," he writes, "commences my first trouble and anxiety as a Shipmaster, having under my charge a valuable vessel and cargo, inexperienced in business, carried into a foreign port, unacquainted with the language, no American Consul or merchant to advise with, and my reputation as a Shipmaster depending upon the measures I pursued."

His papers showing that he was bound for a neutral port had been stolen by the French Prizemaster. Until he got them back, he could do nothing but live on shore and watch his cargo of flour and rice being stolen by the half-starved populace. He consulted the American Chargé d'Affaires in Paris and at the end of six weeks was told that his case had been tried, that the court had decreed that the *Jane* was indeed a neutral vessel, that he was entitled to have her back, and should be paid for his stolen cargo and a daily allowance for the time during which his ship was detained. His spirits rose tremendously. They increased still further when, after three days of dickering, the Agent of Marine agreed to pay for the vanished cargo three times what it had cost in Boston.

His cheerfulness did not last long. How could payment be made? The law forbade any money to be carried out of France, nor was payment in merchandise possible. After much prolonged discussion Cobb agreed to accept government bills of exchange payable in currency in Hamburg sixty days after they had been delivered to him in France. These, it was promised, would be forthcoming within two weeks. Cobb waited a month. Then he sent the *Jane* home in ballast in charge of his mate. He himself, armed with pistols and a blunderbuss, boarded a bullet-proof mail coach bound for the French capital, and after three days and nights of constant vigilance, arrived in Paris to carry his case to headquarters.

There the authorities claimed they had no knowledge of any court decree in his favor, though the official papers had been posted to them days before Cobb left Brest. He pulled out his own official copy and made them look it over. The next day he was informed that the document had been lost. At this desperate moment he determined to take his case directly to Robespierre himself, then in supreme power and supposed to have friendly feelings towards Americans. So Cobb promptly sat down and wrote Robespierre a note. Within an hour a messenger returned with the reply, "I will grant Citizen Cobb an interview tomorrow at ten a.m. Robespierre."

The youth from Cape Cod, face to face with the great master of the Reign of Terror, told his story in detail and promptly won complete support. Robespierre ruled that Cobb should have his bills of exchange immediately. Now under the terms of the agreement he was to receive a daily allowance, or "demurrage," until the time when the bills of exchange were placed in his hands. They were not payable in Hamburg for sixty days, you remember, so the Yankee trader arranged to have the bills sent to his agent at Brest and he himself took time off to see the sights of Paris—at the expense of the French government!

They were gruesome sights. Within three weeks he

watched a thousand persons mount the scaffold to the guillotine, including Robespierre himself. The death of this fearsome dictator caused financial convulsions which brought Cobb's bills on Hamburg to half their face value. He decided to go to Hamburg himself to drive a better bargain. This he certainly did, for in spite of further complications he collected payment in full for the par value of his bills.

When he got back to Boston, he found himself hailed as an authority on collecting debts in Europe. He was in fact the first Yankee captain who had successfully traded with the French under the Reign of Terror. Owners sought him out eagerly to command their cargos. He had only four days with his family at Brewster on Cape Cod and then was off again to sell another cargo in France, where it was still against the law to take currency out of the country. After months of delay he got one-third of his price in silver ingots, deposited in London, and two-thirds in the shape of 40,000 pieces of French silver which he promptly changed for 3,000 Spanish gold doubloons. These, in spite of suspicious searching by French officials, he smuggled out of France and took back to Boston.

Such were the first of many adventures, trading in strange ports, sometimes running into the British blockade. An amusing escapade was his selling against the law eight hogs-heads of rum to the Irish. But on July 5, 1812, Cobb set sail from Cadiz to Boston ignorant of the fact that war had been declared. His ship was captured by the English and he was taken as a prisoner to St. Johns. He seems to have had a rather pleasant sojourn with his British captors, who shared the Cape Cod view that "Mr. Madison's war," as the Cape called it, was only a silly mistake.

However, after he was exchanged, the War of 1812 did keep Captain Elijah Cobb at home while hostilities lasted. Later he made several voyages to Europe and in 1818 embarked on a new venture, the African trade, to Prince's Island in the Gulf of Guinea, one of the worst fever holes of the world. He loaded his ship *The Ten Brothers* with print goods, tobacco, trinkets, and salt beef and brought back palm oil, gold dust, ivory, and coffee. The voyage was so profitable that he returned to the Gulf of Guinea and there met stark tragedy. Two other Cape captains and many in their crews were dying of the fever. Cobb was the only shipmaster in the port who lived to get home. After this, he did not voyage again.

Because Elijah Cobb left his memoirs, we can know him well and live with him through his wily maneuvering, his astute Yankee bargaining, his courage, and enterprise; but he was only one of many. Hundreds of Yankee sea captains and traders were almost as able as Cobb. With such shrewd, courageous, and enterprising sons to start her on the way the young nation could not fail to rise swiftly in commerce, shipping, and power.

It might be well for Americans today, who tend to pamper their children, to think about Elijah Cobb and the many American youths like him who shared, if not shouldered, family burdens from childhood and learned young how to strike a good bargain and carry through a bold adventure.

75

WHY WORK? SOME THOUGHTS

OF AN UNPRACTICAL IDEALIST

ᛒᛒ Written in 1958, in the midst of much discussion about "labor."

SOME years ago I had to call at an office of the Southern Pacific Railroad in Los Angeles to change a ticket. The man at the window transacted the business so swiftly and politely that as I thanked him I said jokingly, "This is certainly a great railroad!" A gleam came into his eye and warmth into his voice. "*We* think," he announced proudly, "that it's the *greatest railroad in the world.*"

That man is having fun out of his work, I thought as I walked away. He feels he's part of a big team which does a real service to the nation, and even as a very small cog in its great machine, he's proud of his place on the team and gets sound satisfaction out of making it an even better railroad.

I thought of him again one night last winter, just before Christmas. There was a blizzard, and at the evening rush hour the Long Island Railroad employees chose that moment to spring a "wildcat" strike. Thousands and thousands of wretched commuters crowded the New York station, most of them weary, wet, and hungry, with no idea how long the "strike" would last, whether they would get home at all that night. What must the ill and the old and the little children have endured! And what conceivably could *they* do to remedy the grievances of the strikers, about which they knew nothing? Why take it out on them? Those railway men, I felt sure, could *not* have been getting much fun or satisfaction out of their work, or realized its human purpose.

I speculated also about the workers in an entirely different field, when I read not very long ago in the morning paper the headline "MET CURTAIN RUNG DOWN AS BALLET RUNS OVERTIME." The article described the chagrin of the prima ballerina, whose artistic sense was naturally outraged when her performance was cut short before it ended. I gathered that the stagehands, the engineers, and others of the unionized staff of the Metropolitan Opera House have to be paid heavy extra rates for any overtime, and that the performance of ballets, though artistically highly desirable, is financially so precarious that the management of this special ballet season does not dare to risk incurring a large additional expense. So they have to sacrifice art.

I wondered how the stagehands, engineers, and others of the Metropolitan felt about this. Do they work solely to earn money for themselves and their families? Do they not take any real interest in the purpose of what they are doing? It would be so much more fun, I should think, for the stagehands, the engineers, and others of the Metropolitan if they felt a deep interest and pride in the production of

77

great operas and ballets. They might then really enjoy contributing a half hour of overtime to round out a fine performance to a culmination of perfection. Thus they might share some of the satisfaction experienced over the years by members of the acting profession, who in face of personal tragedies and financial collapses lived up so long to the fine old tradition "the show must go on."

The show must go on, the house must be built sound and weatherproof, the class must be taught, the sick must be cared for, news of the world must reach us, crime must be stopped—ends such as these are purposes for which we work. If somehow each worker can be conscious of the ultimate purpose and see himself as one part, small perhaps but essential, in the great effort which is going to achieve the purpose, then can we not all lead happier and more satis-fying lives? This joy in team effort for a good end is one of the best reasons for working.

But labor unions, with all their merits, have done much to take away this good reason for working. The workman is forced to be more interested in shortening his hours of work or getting amply paid for overtime than in helping to pro-duce a great performance of a great play. Well do I know how the unions can defend themselves against this charge, how they can point out that they are very necessary in order to protect their men against exploitation by managers and by artists. Of course, there is much to be said for the need of organized effort to advance the interests of laborers; but the unions have come to stress too much the self-interest of those who work and to force them to neglect or be blind to the ultimate fine purpose of the task. The trade union spirit seems to have broken down very largely the old sense of service to a craft, to a skill, to a company, to a community, to the public.

A public service like a railway has as its main purpose the efficient transportation of passengers and freight. In performing this service to the community effectively a good many railway workers still have, I hope, some pride in their roads, parlous though the situation of railways is at the moment, and an eagerness to carry on their share of the duty well and thus serve the public. But the union in seeking its aims has to place above this service to the community the obtaining of shorter hours, higher wages, pensions, and many special benefits for the union members. It must train them to put their own personal interests above their duty of service to the public.

Indeed, the terrible weapon of the strike, as vicious in its way as war itself, obliges railway workers at times to try to prevent by force the carrying out of that public service to which they presumably are dedicated. That is, they must stop the railways from running, block the transportation of passengers and freight, violently prevent other workers from carrying out the tasks that they lay down, thus penalizing the helpless public for grievances for which they are not responsible or to secure personal advantages which the public is helpless to grant. It is almost as if a doctor, dissatisfied with the treatment accorded to him by a hospital or a department of health, should take it out on his helpless patients, neglecting, harming, even killing those for whom he had sworn to care, who are in no way responsible for his own grievances.

All this applies of course equally to other forms of transportation such as planes, ships, and busses and to all public services essential to the men and women and children of our communities. What is becoming of the old feeling of responsibility and pride in performing these services loyally and well even in the face of danger? Some of it remains, of course. I still read of telephone operators who risk their lives staying at their posts through flood and fire.

Not only labor unions but also American parents are to blame for promoting the wrong attitude towards team work for good ends. They stimulate it early in our American children by the unfortunate modern practice of paying them money for doing household chores. If there is any enterprise in which the spirit of "team play," of unselfish devotion to a loved purpose should prevail, surely it is the creation and conduct of the home, which is the focus of the affection of all the family, the center of their common destiny. A child used to be happy and proud when he grew old enough to help mother and father, even in a tiny way, maintain and improve and beautify the home. But nowadays Jimmy or Mary expects to be paid for mowing the lawn or washing the dishes. It seems to them perfectly natural and proper for mother to toil countless hours unpaid over the housework for *their* welfare—but for them to help, oh no, not without cash! They have not learned to feel the common purpose of it all.

When I protest about this practice and say that if children are paid for household chores, then they should have to pay board, harassed American parents just look puzzled and annoyed and reply that they have to follow the customs of the other families in their community.

But team play towards a good end is not the whole picture. The vast majority of jobs of work have involved—and I hope may continue to involve—the exercise of some individual skill. The skills vary immensely in kind and degree, as does the personal satisfaction derived from employing them.

Contemplate the clam-digger on the sands. Some joy of the hunt as well as his "feel" of the ways of clams gives tang to his work. Imagine also the intense concentration of a surgeon at the operating table whose hands, brain, and wisdom born of years of experience carry him on through hours of a delicate operation on which a human life depends. Picture young Van Cliburn at the piano, after years of assiduous practice and performance, playing the Tchaikovsky Concerto before that great Moscow assemblage, feeling his hands, his brain, his imagination, all merging with the sympathetic response of his vast audience and creating a pinnacle of artistic emotion. And think of Einstein looking upon the formula produced by his brain, his pencil, and his paper, the brief formula which explains the mechanism of the universe.

Such exercise of personal skill is "work." It is also the breath of life. Some similar sense of gratification and release innumerable other workers get from exercising their own skills, whatever they may be. This is perhaps the most potent of all reasons for working.

The artisan can often feel some of the satisfaction of the artist, but not as much as in past ages. The mechanization and standardization of industry leave little to the initiative and skill of the individual craftsman. Never again, it seems, can a stonecutter be blessed with the freedom and joy which were granted to his fellow of the Middle Ages who himself created while with his own hand he executed the delightful, the humorous, the beautiful figures which adorned the medieval cathedrals.

Another influence tends to rob the artisan of pleasure—the trade union spirit, which often seems to try to reduce all workmen to a dead level of mediocrity. A bricklayer is limited in the number of bricks he may lay in a day. Gone is much of the joy and pride in his skill. And more and more will "automation" reduce us to mere button-pushers. But if not in our paid work for a livelihood, still in our pastimes in hours of leisure we may enjoy the sense of power and skill in the deft turn of the hand.

As for the professions, most professional workers who deserve the name follow their profession because they love it. They do not need to be told *why* they should work. From the exercise of their professional skill they derive profound satisfaction. I observe that this is true of many physicians, engineers, and architects. Of as large a proportion of lawyers? I do not know.

Of my own profession, teaching, it is often true. For the

born teacher nothing can give more satisfaction than teaching. But, alas, many who teach are not born teachers, and the circumstances of the work often make it drudgery, and underpaid drudgery at that. So that at times teaching is slipping from the status of a profession to that of a trade. Teachers have felt driven to organize pressure groups and even to *strike*. Appalling thought!

Since I retired from my active life as teacher and administrator I have dabbled just a very little in another profession —that of author. But that ranks with the arts. Real writers, like painters, sculptors, and musicians, practice their art because they must. Poor things, their inner urge forces them to write, and as very few can possibly earn a living at it they are obliged to do some other work for bread and butter.

Well, why not? Walter de la Mare, I believe, held some post in the Bank of England, probably a dull, bleak one, and produced his delightful poems in what we might call his hours of leisure. That adjustment of one's life will probably become more and more common in future. Our real "work," our principal contribution to society, to civilization, will often be done in our time of "leisure."

Another excellent reason for working is that it makes leisure so much more fun. Even if you love your work, there are bound to be stretches of drudgery in it and periods of long strain and fatigue. Then, if you feel you have really been doing a good job and accomplished a bit, what a pleasure it is to stop, to relax and rest and turn to play!

What to do with our supposedly increasing leisure is, however, a problem that stimulates much discussion today. With the development of mechanization and automation, we are told, not merely the four-day week but perhaps the *four-hour* week looms in the near future. In that brief spell of labor a factory worker may earn enough to support himself and his family. But what will he do with the rest of his time? Fill a good part of it, if he be sensible, with some self-chosen work. Otherwise "leisure" for most people will certainly have lost its tang. As Clifton Fadiman once said, "It doesn't take a psychologist to predict that if we try to fill this leisure by putting a small white ball into a slightly larger hole or gawking at television crooners, we will as a people go quietly or noisily nuts."

The prospect is really not as black as it is sometimes painted. In the first place this four-hour or even four-day week will never apply to professional workers and artists, who will surely go on working as hard as ever, filling in their "leisure" with gardening or golf or reading or music or community affairs or with that occupation now forced willy-nilly on the professional and all other classes—helping with the housework.

The other workers, if loaded with a vast surplus of "non-working" hours, will have to turn to larger doses of hobbies and handicrafts. But they certainly will have to include in these, for real satisfaction, as I have suggested, some one thing requiring strenuous and continued effort, actual "work." For most men like to work, contrary to popular belief. They even like their jobs, some recent statistics show, and must find some compensating substitute for them if that four-hour week ever actually arrives. The psychiatrists will agree, for they still prescribe for the proper life, I believe, a balanced program of work, play, and rest. Take away the work and the foundation of your structure is gone.

At this point most readers are probably annoyed because so far, save for casual allusions, I have omitted what seems to them the main, often the only, reason for working—that is, to earn a living for yourself and those dependent on you. Well, of course that is still for most of us a fundamental reason, though in the welfare state it may be becoming less and less urgent.

Hungry children can stir nearly any father or mother to eager "toil and sweat." From food on up through a hundred gadgets to mink coats and other badges of social status there are personal and family needs and desires that spur men and women on to work. The consciousness that you are providing some of them for your wife and children, or your mother, or your invalid husband, must be a very great consolation and satisfaction to those unfortunates whose work in itself gives no gratification or who are working under bullying bosses or in other painful circumstances.

To put it rather differently, readers may bitterly complain that I have omitted the most plain, obvious reason for working—to earn money! Earning money is, of course, a necessity for the vast majority of us. It is also the great American game. Your success in life, especially in the business world, is most often measured by the amount of money you have made; it is like achieving a top score in golf. And it is not just money, it is *power* that you win in this great competitive American game. Fortunately it does not appeal to all of us, or many delightful jobs, such as that of archae-ologist and research philologist, would go unfilled. I recall a dear friend of mine, dead these many years, who when offered a position in an insurance company far more lucra-tive than his school-mastering, just murmured gently, "No. Thank you very much. I think the Lord intended me to teach small boys."

I certainly do not expect to lure many from the great money-making game, or to alter the economic structure of our time. But I deeply believe we must try to preserve and to respect some of the other reasons for working, and thus add to human happiness. Of course we must have labor unions; of course we cannot turn the clock back; of course stone-cutters can no longer create from their own free fan-cies beauty, grotesqueness, humor, as they did at Chartres; of course we do not want to exchange our family Ford for the buckboard and ponies of my youth. But as we undergo the inevitable changes in our social, our economic, our me-chanical mode of life, we should try to cling to at least a fraction of the good things, the deeply heartening things of the old order. So I plead for a sense of the joy of work, the team play towards a good end, service to the community, the profound satisfaction of using one's skill, perhaps to create a bit of beauty, perhaps to give ease from pain, per-haps just to bring the healthy sense of fatigue and sweat on the brow after an honest spell of physical toil.

Written in 1958.

THE small boy looked up at the tall artist he had met on the Roman Road in the English countryside. "And all the knights who were brave and tried so hard but who never killed a dragon or won a tournament or even married a second-class princess, *they*'ll be there, won't they?" he asked. They were discussing a delightful and consoling subject: a city in the clouds where there would live happily small boys who were not understood at home and artists who never quite achieved the vision of which they dreamed and many others who somehow did not attain the goal at which they aimed, or, having attained it, found themselves robbed of all the glory of it and that glory given to undeserving rivals.

Whenever I recall that charming story in one of the most charming of books, Kenneth Grahame's *Golden Age*, I find myself thinking of Sir Clamados of the Shadows. During my youth I spent many happy hours wandering through the mysterious forests of the Arthurian legend in Malory and other romances, where Launcelot and Gawaine and Bors and Perceval and many another gallant knight rode to high adventure and slew the wicked and rescued the fair and crashed to victory in the lists and won great renown.

Among all these brilliant heroes I have been haunted by another figure, a vague one whom I met occasionally, always striving valiantly for high emprise worthy of his knighthood, for good deeds and fair fame, but always failing, his stout heart and generous spirit ever thwarted by ill fortune. He was Sir Clamados, son of the Lord of the Forest of the Shadows. He flits a few times briefly through the Arthurian story. For fifty years I have thought of him and intended to write of him, because, though he himself has slipped vaguely back into the shadows, I have known and heard through my life of others like him, as brave and worthy as Launcelot himself but splintering their spears in vain against persistent and malevolent ill fortune.

Like the small boy on the Roman Road I must have had an early and instinctive sympathy and liking for the knight who was always unhorsed in the lists, for whose victory the trumpets never blared. I have remembered with approval the remark made to me long ago by an older friend of mine, Adrian Joline: "The finest men are not always the successful ones. Think of Hamlet and Brutus."

Most of all, this odd instinct of mine—which is not just natural sympathy for the underdog—is shown by the admiration and sense of belonging which I felt as an undergraduate when I first read Matthew Arnold's lovely invocation to Oxford, as "she lies, spreading her gardens to the moonlight . . . . home of lost causes, and forsaken beliefs, and unpopular names, and impossible loyalties!" Noble and fine such a center of learning seemed to me. I would proudly have joined that fellowship. And a thousand times since my undergraduate days I have repeated to myself those noble words.

"Odd" I have called this instinct of mine, because in my own personal life up to my seventieth year, with a few tragic exceptions good fortune followed me with amazing persistence and victory perched upon the banners of the causes for which I worked, or at least seemed to perch there.

Meanwhile this quirk of mind helped me to hold out against the glamor or popularity of some of the great figures and ideas of my time, often to form my own opinion of what was true or just or beautiful irrespective of popular clamor. Most of the causes which I adopted happened to be on the road up at the moment or soon to become so. But I do not think that I ever refused to support what seemed to me a good cause just because people told me it was an absolutely hopeless one.

So I happily campaigned for "Al" Smith, to the horror of my Republican friends, when he sought the presidency in 1928. So for thirty years I struggled in an increasingly vain effort to preserve the study of the classics, especially Greek. And so in my later life I have fought against powerful and ruthless pressures for what seemed to me to lead to peace with justice in the Middle East. Sir Clamados and other shadowy knights of my past have ridden forth to sustain me and cheer me on my way.

The bright radiance of success so often blinds people's eyes to real values. It is worthwhile to stress again the need to penetrate through success and seek the merits of those men and those causes that at the moment are caught at the bottom of the Wheel of Fortune. Just plain bad luck can strike down the best of us.

In my professional work as college administrator, in dealing with professors and students and alumnae, in trying to secure a high reputation for my college and adequate funds, I had of course to emphasize success, to cherish and support especially successful teachers and scholars and the most promising young students, make them appear interesting and glamorous to the world. I never fell into the grave error of spending most of my efforts on the lame ducks or the unfortunate.

But Sir Clamados always lurked in the back of my mind. As colleges go I think ours was fairly considerate of those pursued by ill luck. I remember setting up with the help of my kindly and generous friend Mrs. Frederic Lee a little fund to assist students whose academic records were so bad that they did not qualify even for a "grant-in-aid" but who had had such persistent ill luck that we felt they never had a chance to show their possible ability. "The fund for the undeserving poor" we privately called it. And I remember President Butler's wise saying: "Surely the last time to cut a professor's salary is when he is ill."

Life in academic halls is not usually considered highly adventurous and chancy, but it can be so. The fickle goddess Fortune, who frowned upon Sir Clamados in the Forest of the Shadows, can also frustrate and strike down a gifted young scholar entering upon a career of college teaching in a "cockpit of learning," as one of the great Harvard departments was once called. Comparing my own long stretch of good luck with the experience of others, I can see the pitfalls of chance that await him. He, or more often she, may prove so useful an assistant that his seniors, themselves growing old and in need of support, may hold him on for years as helper with promises of future reward which they are powerless to fulfill. The fields of his subject for which the young scholar has been especially trained at the highest source may just happen to be covered by older teachers who stay on and on, or given for inadequate reasons to less qualified members of the staff.

The caliber of personality of those in administrative power over him may be poor—negligent, biased, or even jealous of youthful success. So also with his other seniors and colleagues. Luck plays a fateful part in determining the quality of the persons with whom your life happens to be cast.

Death, poverty, and similar family tragedies may strike at critical moments. War may call him to national service. Depressions may block the college budget and prevent advancement just when he might secure it; so may faculty politics and intrigue. And finally the cruel clutch of disease may cut short his gallant effort.

These pieces of ill fortune strike here and there in a college staff. Strangely enough I have seen them all pursue a single individual, one of the most brilliant young teachers and scholars I have ever known, a quite incredible run of bad luck. Should we value him the less because public success rarely favored him?

Nor is it only in college faculties that unjust fates pursue the gifted. When in Rome I visited an honored grave and read upon the stone only the words "Here lies one who writ in water," I felt a shock of surprise. I had of course known for many years that the embittered young poet had asked that this inscription be placed on his tomb, but somehow had not quite realized that the illustrious and much-loved name John Keats had actually been omitted.

> O what can ail thee, knight-at-arms,
>   Alone and palely loitering?
> The sedge is wither'd from the lake,
>   And no birds sing!

Was Keats portraying in these words a shadowy figure like my Sir Clamados or was he portraying himself? For surely no man exemplifies better than he the tragic course of ill fortune. Dying at twenty-five, the young poet looked back upon birth in an unpromising setting, an inadequate education, an uncongenial apprenticeship to a surgeon, sneering and damning reviews of his early poems, a hopeless passion over years for a woman he could never marry, a long and fatal illness of tuberculosis.

I owned for a while a water-color sketch by his friend Arthur Severn, made from life of him as he sat on the deck of the *Maria Crowther* sailing from England for the last time. He looked so ill, so young, so broken. He could not know that posterity would grant him fame, would place the quality of some of his verse even with Shakespeare's. What might he not have given us in his later years if Fortune had granted him a more fostering life? What may we not have lost from the pens of other poets who could not withstand even as long as did Keats the buffets of scorn and ill luck, whose spirits broke earlier under the ordeal?

Whenever I look at the "best seller" lists I think of John Keats, who would never have been on one. Surely they bring too much glamor to a few and help block the paths of many others equally gifted. They are a part of the whole vast pattern of publicity and public relations which dominates so much of our life today, often dangerously. The elaborate apparatus of the "Madison Avenue Boys" now competes with the goddess Fortune in determining the success or failure of men. It can raise up some and strike down others.

We have all seen this great machine operating in recent years at election time. Of course, in a democracy where offices are filled by popular vote, the outward aspect, the charm, the dramatic circumstances of candidates have always influenced the final choice. Now this influence has been increased a hundredfold. Attainment of high office often seems to depend largely on the skill of the public relations firms employed and on the amount of money available to buy time and space on radio, television, and press. Most perilous of all, the preliminary choice of a candidate may be determined by his suitability for such exploitation rather than by his fundamental character and ability. (I do not mean to imply that outward charm never accompanies inner competence and soundness. Happily they are sometimes combined in one individual.)

Not only in politics does this "personality" emphasis prevail. For some years important posts at the head of institutions and organizations have often been given by trustees and other authorities to candidates glamorous in outward aspect and charming in manner, rather than to those with the fundamental abilities and character needed for the job. If I have protested, the authorities have generally said, "Oh, never mind administrative ability! Others can do the actual administration. We need *him* as a public figure, a front, to attract public interest and support." But that sort of setup rarely works. After all, if the "front" has the post and the power, the welfare and lives of thousands are subject to his will, and who knows when or how he will exert it? Meanwhile, wiser and worthier leaders have been left behind in the Forest of the Shadows, sometimes wounded grievously by the poisoned arrows of the conflict.

Since 1952 there has often floated in my mind with Sir Clamados—*absit omen!*—another knightly figure. He appeared suddenly in that year to a people in confusion, deeply in need of leadership. To many of us he seemed an answer to prayer, a man of vision, courage, brains, knowledge, humor, and eloquence. Surely he was destined at some time to lead his country out of the bogs of confusion and incompetence! But I fear the goddess Fortune has been against him. He just happened to be running for the presidency on the two occasions when a great war hero, to whose name everyone rallied, was the opposing candidate. It just happened in the second campaign that a grave international crisis and danger of war struck during the hectic week preceding Election Day, and Americans instinctively clung to

94

their old practice of not changing horses in midstream.

Overwhelmingly defeated, can this new knight ever ride again? Will a turn of Fortune's wheel bring Adlai Stevenson forth into the sunshine, to give his talents to his country, serving her in some high emprise?

In the Forest of the Shadows rest obscurely many whose courage, brains, and skill might in the past have given America, had she known and used them, the kind of leadership she has often desperately needed and still desperately needs. But they were wasted. Can she in the future somehow manage to pierce the shadows which may veil the talents of some of her most gifted sons?

MEDITATIONS ON THE CAPE

RABBIT

This little friendly greeting to some of our four-footed neighbors was written in 1957 for the *Cape Cod Compass,* an annual which is published by two enterprising and plucky Cape women and to which many authors resident on the Cape contribute.

HAVE you ever seen a youngish rabbit sitting on the lawn spring suddenly straight up into the air vertically, like a helicopter, only much faster? It's a sign of exuberance in him, I am sure, and it lifts my spirits, too. To leap vertically is impossible for the next-size younger rabbits, who just jump gaily over each other's backs, weaving to and fro in a playful dance, and certainly for the very wee ones, who merely nibble the greenest grass and twinkle their noses. The elderly rabbits, too, like us humans in our later years, leap straight skyward no more.

My life with the Cape rabbits is passed as I lie for many hours in a long chair on a lawn under a huge, very ancient willow, looking out to sea. While I am alone and motionless the rabbits tolerate me and go about their noiseless lives around me. They are pleasant companions but never become close friends, as did the grey squirrels long ago in Riverside Park, New York. I'd much rather be a squirrel, for unlike the timid, perpetually alarmed rabbit he leads a bold, adventurous life, rejoicing in running down the tree trunk almost to the nose of his enemy, the leaping, barking dog, chattering defiantly and sometimes jumping off to the ground right under the dog's open mouth and darting to the next tree with gay bravado. He is the greatest leaper I ever beheld, yet I never saw him undertake that straight, helicopter lift.

The Skipper, with whom I live, thinks I underrate the spirit of the Cape rabbit. She assures me she once saw one actually chasing a squirrel, and another bold, sturdy individualist leap out of the bushes and start in pursuit of a young, miniature black poodle, who turned tail and scurried, panic-stricken, towards his home.

But my rabbits are bold only in nibbling off the young petunias we try to grow to make a splash of color by our front door. When I see them thus marauding I shout and drive them off. It's a hopeless battle, for in the early mornings I'm not in the long chair and they have a free field.

Daily they munch the seedlings, and if by some extraordinary chance a few plants live to grow large, our rabbits also enjoy beating down the blossoming, spreading petunia branches, using them as beds at night, crushing them comfortably flat. Moth balls judiciously scattered are said to prevent this, but I have doubted it profoundly ever since I saw a baby rabbit playing with one of the moth balls, as a puppy would with a rubber ball, pushing it with his nose, rolling it down the slope of the lawn, drawing back in pretended fright and then nosing it again.

A more drastic way of limiting the depredations of rabbits is provided by a family of foxes which has established itself in a copse at the end of the lawn near the water. The young foxes sometimes come out and play on the grass by moonlight, circling each other with high capers, seeming to dance. I fear their larder is supplied largely by our rabbits, who tend to avoid that part of the lawn, but not always successfully.

In spite of this peril the race will probably survive for ages to come, unless that deadly plague which, I am told, has exterminated the rabbits of England, penetrates Cape Cod. Our Cape rabbits, with their charming white "scuts," unlike most of the rabbits of America, are descended from English rabbits brought over by our first settlers. I knew their English cousins well, though not so intimately, for I watched them during the many summers I spent in a cottage on the South Downs in Sussex between the two World Wars. The English took their rabbits hard. Instead of spreading the lawn and flower beds hospitably open, as we Americans do, an English cottage made itself a fortress against rabbit attack. Our acre on the South Downs had all around it a high, stout hedge, reinforced by chicken wire three feet up and two feet underground. In spite of this a small rabbit sometimes slipped through a gate and when seen caused alarums and excursions in the household until he was driven out.

On my daily walks over the Downs, however, I saw multitudes of rabbits, source of endless excitement and joy to our terriers. There was a rabbit warren on the side of a lower outcrop of the Down, with scores of rabbit holes into which the residents whisked hastily as we approached. It was a sort of City of Rabbits, where they enjoyed, I hope, a happy community life.

The frantic pursuits by our dogs were almost always harmless, but once my White Highland terrier Jean actually caught and killed a baby rabbit, which she proudly tried to present to me. She was very hurt in spirit when I unjustly repulsed her with indignant reproaches.

Occasionally I met at the foot of the Downs a man with a "lurcher"—a rather large greyhound-like dog whose slim body and long legs made him death to the rabbits our short-legged terriers could not harm. Then I opined I had met a poacher, and all the long tradition of poachers in English literature rose in my mind. For when a villager killed a rabbit in England it was apparently poaching and subject to punishment, unlike our Cape hunting. But in one way or another rabbits got into the pots of many Sussex peasant homes.

When I visited my cottage briefly after World War II, there was scarcely a rabbit to be seen—the beleaguered Britons had had to eat them to keep fed through those terrible years. Then the rabbits began to multiply once more, but the dread plague crept over from France and exterminated all English rabbits, I read, though rumor says some remain in Scotland and Wales.

Suppose the blight falls on our Cape rabbits. Shall we rejoice at being freed from the damaging pests gardeners have cursed so long? Perhaps. But a few of us will feel bereft, somehow a little lonelier. My lawn will be much less full of life, as I lie in the long chair.

And before they go, if go they must, it would be nice really to know the private life of the rabbit—not hutch-housed and penned, but wild rabbits in their natural homes. From the number of tiny ears one discovers pushing up through the uncut grass each season, I gather that the cycle of life moves fast. Are mating and babies and daytime snoozing all that goes on down in a rabbit hole? Was the City of Rabbits on the English Downs, are the warrens under my Cape cliff capable of any activities akin to the social excitement of the underground life of the ant? Has anyone succeeded in slicing down through the warrens and watching life there in such a way that the timid occupants are not aware of observers? If so, and it must be so, I have not happened to read any account of rabbits relaxed, rabbits not chewing, rabbits at peace, unafraid.

And if the silent, shy marauders are doomed to disappear, what will take the place of that look of delight and enchanted wonder that comes into the eyes of a child when it first discovers a rabbit?

OBNOXIOUS NEUTRALITY?

❦❦ Written in 1958 and published in slightly abbreviated form in the *Saturday Review* for May 10, 1958. Deeply interested for many years in the relationship of nations, watching closely and sometimes participating in the efforts to bring about international understanding and world order, I found the acute anxiety of my country about "neutralism" in others an intriguing subject. It had not, I felt, been thought out clearly, and so in this essay I tried to make a start on the problem.

I AM continually irritated by the American attitude about neutrality. Americans are so smug and virtuous about it, as if they were the only people to whom it had ever occurred that war is a brutal and futile thing, and as if we in Europe all enjoyed it and did it to amuse ourselves."

Am I dreaming, thought I? Can anyone really have said this about Americans? I looked at the date on the letter from my English friend Caroline Spurgeon, which I had found on going over some old papers. The date was October 1, 1939, a month after Hitler invaded Poland and the worst of all wars had begun. She was writing from Tucson, Arizona, where she was living for reasons of health and where she was surrounded by friendly Americans "so smug and virtuous" about their neutrality.

What a contrast to the present anxious attitude of my fellow Americans! They now view with suspicion and fear what they tend to call "neutralism," bitterly resentful of nations like India, who cannot distinguish between black and white and so do not definitely side with us in the Cold War with Russia; shocked and alarmed by a recent world poll of public opinion which showed that only two of the eleven Western nations tested would favor entering a war to help us fight the Reds.

The variety of emotions with which the American people have regarded this concept is duplicated in an amusing way by the history of the word *neutral* and its derivatives as recorded in the fascinating depths of the Oxford Dictionary. The word *neuter*, akin to *neither*, early appears as meaning not only *of neither sex* but in general *neither one thing nor its opposite*.

Sometimes it has signified a *good* thing. Note "such as are neutrals, who may labor with the one side and the other to compound the quarrel"; "their neutralism will be at an end, denominationalism will have made them prisoners"; "the largest and best minds . . . arrive at a sort of neutral region."

But the concept of *indifference* early casts a shadow on the word: witness "a neuter town indifferent to both" and "unkindness of neuterlike indifference." More unfavorable connotations appear in such statements as "in politics they are a breed of mongrels or neutrals"; "our own neutralism and lukewarmness shall utterly condemn us"; "the profane neutralist who is of all religions or no religion"; "the silent neutralist soon became regarded as the secret foe"; "I had a neutralizing spirit—I looked which way the wind blew."

My thoughts run back all the long years during which I have watched American minds and hearts sway violently "which way the wind blew," reaching opposite poles in their attitude toward neutrality. They have been driven hither and thither by changing circumstances, which now made neutrality a refuge in which we could preserve our own civilization and way of thinking and save our own skins, and then caused it to appear to be a horrid disease, a kind of moral blindness which afflicted other nations and kept them from standing by our side to help us.

What is the truth about it all? Should we really try to stamp out neutrality as thoroughly obnoxious, or should we aim for a world where everyone is neutral and so at peace?

When World War I burst upon our amazed country, President Woodrow Wilson urged us all to be neutral in thought as well as in deed. The great majority of Americans certainly wanted to keep out of the horrible and confusing European madness. We wrapped our oceans about us and withdrew to our hereditary isolation. Mr. Wilson won re-election with the slogan, "He Kept Us Out of War."

But Theodore Roosevelt said, "Dante reserved a special place of infamy in the inferno for those base angels who dared side neither with evil nor with good. Peace is ardently to be desired, but only as the handmaid of righteousness." Gradually we felt a changing of the national emotions. The sinking of the *Lusitania* and of other ships which brought death to some American citizens aroused our anger and indignation. We also resented the edicts of Germany which limited the sailing of our ships and so deprived us of our ancient freedom of the seas. "No, Mr. Kaiser," one furious old sea-captain was reported to have declared, "we will *not* paint our ships like barberpoles and sail them only once a week!"

Many of us began to feel uneasy about President Wilson's statement that we were "too proud to fight." Was that really as noble as it had seemed at first? Were we not responsible citizens of the world? Was it not our duty to try to restore peace—and a peace with justice? Was it not even conceivably possible that the forces of violence and evil might threaten our own shores and the security of our own quiet homes? Were we not playing a pusillanimous part in just sitting on the sidelines, making vast sums of money out of the sufferings of other nations, and doing nothing to stop the holocaust?

Unlimited submarine warfare and the revelation of a message from Germany promising Mexico the restoration of her "lost province" of Texas (You should have seen the expression on the faces of the Texans!) helped fire American emotions to the boiling point, so that we were willing to drop the neutrality which we had cherished and enter on a crusade for peace. We would fight "to make the world safe for democracy." This war would end all wars. Away with that feeble thing, neutrality! We became belligerents.

The results of our crusade disillusioned us bitterly. Internal partisan politics confused the issues. We were disgusted by European politics. We were outmaneuvered at the treaty tables. We refused to join the League of Nations which we had sponsored. Again isolation seemed to us very attractive and the emotions of the American people swung again toward neutrality. "Let's keep out of it all!"

As the black clouds of World War II gathered on the horizon, we were grimly determined to avoid being entangled again in these world politics which disgusted and puzzled us. This time we would not be caught! Congress passed drastic neutrality legislation forbidding American citizens to enter the area of war, forbidding American ships to sail into war zones. Soon however we became outraged by Hitler's persecutions of the Jews. We were frightened by his conquest of the European continent. What would be the results to us of a Hitler victory? We envisaged the possible extinction of England and France, our fellow democracies. Many patriotic American citizens had favored isolation, but they had not anticipated an isolation like this, when, alone in the world, the United States would face world forces of tyranny and evil.

Franklin Roosevelt, convinced that our real interests lay in preserving a world-neighborhood of "decent" nations, stretched neutrality almost to the breaking point by selling fifty destroyers to the British and by setting up the system of "lend lease" to supply the Allies. Many of us supported him enthusiastically. I remember being a member of the Committee to Defend America by Aiding the Allies, which urged that we should render all help "short of war." In such a conflict no one, we felt, could be really neutral in spirit, even though we clung as long as possible to the legal status.

However, the emotions of the country were seriously divided and at odds. I used to wonder how the terrible issue could be solved, and then Japan solved it for us by the attack on Pearl Harbor. Under that blow the minds and the hearts of Americans became united. We entered World War II.

Since that moment we have not been able to enjoy the blessing of neutrality, if it is a blessing. This second world war left us with such painfully obvious international responsibilities and hazards that isolation was no longer to be dreamed of. We helped build the Charter of the United Nations as an instrument through which to work for human welfare. In its General Assembly, Security Council, and International Court of Justice we hoped to find, not neutrality exactly, but fairness, impartiality, and justice. Then our bright hopes were almost immediately wrecked by the rapid development of the Cold War between the Soviet Union and the United States, with many of the nations of the world lined up on one side or the other as "satellites" or allies.

At first the Cold War did not seem to us so menacing. We had the monopoly of the atomic bomb and thus felt ourselves and our allies protected. But as the ghastly procession of new devices of destruction emerged from research laboratories and factories—the enormously enlarged atomic bomb, the hydrogen bomb, the long-range missile—and when finally the Sputniks began to circle the earth, the possibility of the actual destruction of our globe itself loomed ahead of us and fear chilled the hearts of men. Even our own great country, so confident, so safe for many years, now for the first time faced real fear of destruction. Unused to such danger, we tended to become hysterical. Our very existence was at stake. How could we tolerate neutrality in other countries? He who was not for us was against us!

Unhappily, the growth of this fear in American minds and hearts coincided with an ever-increasing antipathy to the whole business of the Russo-American feud on the part of the other nations of the world. "A plague on both your houses," they ardently wished, and would doubtless have liked to see the two great giants destroy each other completely and leave the rest of the world to peace.

We shall soon learn, I trust, to shed this panicky fear which has afflicted us and live calmly, if necessary, as Finland has for so long and Austria has recently learned so well, under the immediate threat of the paws of the Bear. We must make our power and our brains stronger and more effective, accepting these tensions, adjusting the political and psychological problems of the world on some working basis of tolerance and even cooperation before we blow the globe back into the gaseous vapors from which it emerged so many eons ago.

Meanwhile, remembering our own periods of ardent neutrality, let us try to understand and to respect neutral nations. When I went to Europe at the end of World War II I found that the belligerents, far from reproaching the two neutrals, Sweden and Switzerland, felt warm gratitude to them for their immense help in providing relief for sick children, refugees, and other sufferers in adjacent countries, and for making possible some human communication in a world of hostile barriers through which no friendly words could pass.

Not only Sweden, Switzerland, Finland, and Austria, but even the great neutral nation of India, we must try to understand and respect. We should appreciate, even though we do not agree with Nehru's efforts to follow the spirit of Gandhi and promote an avoidance of all violence in this world of armaments and threats. We must recognize that in the face of her vast problems of poverty, starvation, and misery India must for the present use all her energies for herself. Above all, we should stop sermonizing neutral nations, waving moralizing slogans at them, making statements like that attributed to former President Hoover in his recent denunciation of "neutralism" as, along with "Communism" and "Socialism," an "evil" thing.

Neutrality is by no means always obnoxious. Neutral nations can indeed be of great value to the world and may develop into the leaders in our common struggle toward a world order. Let us not forget that it is Sweden which has given us Dag Hammerskjold, who more than any other single individual was perhaps the greatest force for world peace today. Contemplate more closely that extraordinary small country in the very heart of Europe, most ancient of existing republics—Switzerland. It is so rootedly neutral in legal status that it has even felt unable to join the United Nations. Yet it generously aids the United Nations by giving hospitality to its offices in Geneva; it is the central headquarters of the International Red Cross; and it cooperates in scores of other ways to help solve international problems and ease the sufferings of man. Its highly intelligent citizens, while their nation holds rigidly to its legal neutrality, preserve the freedom of their individual minds and opinions and the warmth of their sympathies. A model neutral is Switzerland!

During the foreseeable future there will continue to be neutral nations, perhaps an increasing number of them, forced into that position by dire pressure of circumstance, or choosing it for philosophical or emotional reasons. But from now on most of the larger nations can rarely be neutral. Certainly that possibility will seldom be open to the United States. As one of the pillars of the United Nations we are often forced to take, in that body, definite stands and even definite actions for or against certain policies and certain nations. Witness Korea, and also the situation which confronted us when Israel, Britain, and France invaded Egypt in 1956. Our country must continue to be an active and responsible citizen of the United Nations world.

Looking toward the long future, perhaps we may venture to hope that codes of world law and even—who knows?—of world ethics may be crystallized and generally accepted. As the organization for world order grows stronger we citizen-nations may come to look upon it as the private citizens of a state look upon their courts and their police and their welfare agencies—free to criticize and grumble at times, but on the whole supporting the world order as man's best chance for peace and well-being.

In that hope we *may* survive through the next decade.

THE TIP ENDS OF THINGS:

JOURNEYS INTO THE REMOTE

🜂🜃 Written in 1957, before the Sputniks opened up so vividly the possibilities of outer space. For many years one of my most enjoyable hobbies was reading books about Polar exploration and other journeys into remote places. This interest hitched up somehow with my taste for archaeology and also with the scholar's search for new knowledge. To stand upon man's outermost footing and reach out into the unknown, that idea has had a kind of mystical attraction for me. This little essay, therefore, is not just a glimpse of arctic adventures but an expression of a side of my mind which I have rarely tried to put into words.

TODAY as I write they are burying at Arlington National Cemetery in Washington with high military honors Richard Byrd. "Admiral of the Arctic Air," we might call him. He was the first man to fly over both the Poles, and I thought of him also a fortnight ago when I read with lively interest and a tinge of regret two Polar news items. The first told how two Scandinavian Airways planes passed each other right over the North Pole, on the first commercial flights of a direct service between Copenhagen and Tokyo. The second described the elaborately equipped winter quarters at the South Pole itself in which eighteen men of the U.S. Navy, from Admiral Byrd's Antarctic Command, are to defy the long winter night on that vast, high plateau, swept by sub-subzero gales and blizzards and ringed by the mountains and glaciers which for so long guarded the southern tip of our globe and kept man at bay. Thus, it seemed to me, modern science has robbed some of the glamor and mystery from two of the remote spots where over many years my adventurous imagination has liked to dwell.

However, I do not intend to give up this pastime, happy refuge after a long day of hard work and immersion in the perplexing, pressing present. I commend such hobbies to others who seek change, variety, a breath of distant adventure. There is something peculiarly exhilarating for those whose bodies can rarely venture far, in reading and dreaming of remote spots on this earth, and especially the tip ends of things from which they can look off beyond man's outermost footing into the unknown.

My favorite tip has long been Attu. One day many years ago I was sitting through a committee meeting in the office, I think, of the Guggenheim Foundation. Opposite me on the wall hung a map of the world. As my eye followed the long, slender finger of the Aleutian Islands, stretching so far, far out from lower Alaska to a point below the Kamchatka Peninsula and way beyond its tip, I thought how exciting it would be to stand on the very last of these islands, the remote and final western boundary of American land,

and look out toward Asia. I do not think that I knew then that its name was Attu.

After that I read with fascinated interest everything I found about the Aleutians, not very much until World War II. Then the Japanese captured Attu and Kiska, and we heard more. I saw photographs of that mountainous and bleak island; I read the story of the American schoolteacher and his wife who were captured there by the Japanese when they first attacked; and once I met a nurse who had been stationed on Attu for a time during the war. As a member of the great Navy family I also heard romantic tales of the setting up of the secret Naval bases in the Aleutians and something of the difficulties of life at the stations there, the boredom and the heroism of the men and their fantastic adventures.

I gather that the Aleutians are a singularly unattractive part of the world. I have had no special desire to experience in person their fogs and "williwaws," but I should certainly like to visit another significant edge in Alaska, that point on Bering Strait where the Continent of Asia and the Continent of North America come nearest together. Standing there on our Alaskan coast on one of the rare fine days and looking out across the fifty-three-mile wide Strait, you can see far to the right the tip of Asia at East Cape, and, to the left, the westernmost reach of North America, Cape Prince of Wales. Between them lie the Diomede Islands. Little Diomede belongs to us, and beyond it, only two and one-half miles away, Big Diomede belongs to the Soviet Union. Rocky, desolate, and remote, that is one of the significant and dramatic meeting places of the world.

The faraway tip of Africa attracts me less, but the south-ernmost point of our own Continent, where Cape Horn rises out of the stormy seas, has always fired my imagination, as it has that of all Americans of maritime descent. I have read the accounts of the first explorers from Magellan on-ward, and have always thought that I should like to visit the dangerous Straits which bear his name; and the perilous Cape around which the beautiful American clipper ships raced to San Francisco and China; and the mysterious land of Tierra del Fuego and that southernmost city of our Con-tinent, Punta Arenas.

Being fond of the contemplation of remote and mysterious places I was, naturally enough, early fascinated by the Poles. That was long before scientific invention had made them almost familiar, as they are today. They were still wrapped in icy barriers, impenetrable to man. From my easy chair in hours of leisure I could accompany the heroes who through the years made attack after attack on these frozen and perilous mysteries. Nansen's great book *Farthest North*, literature as well as adventure, gave me my first thrill of romantic interest in the Arctic. (I was very proud when I met him many years later at Oslo.) Starting with *Farthest North*, I collected a fairly good lot of books on Polar ex-peditions.

Thus I became closely acquainted with the behavior of pack ice, spent the long Arctic night hibernating with Nan-sen and Johansen in their underground stone hut off Franz Josef Land, was puzzled by Dr. Cook's claims, and tri-umphed with Peary. Even more intimate have I felt with the vast Antarctic Continent, its Barrier ice, its frozen mountains, and its lofty gale-swept plateau, forbidding and terrible. At one period during my life I read so many books about the Shackleton, Scott, and Amundsen expeditions that I began to feel quite familiar with the topography of the South Polar land. I used to think that if I were dropped down somewhere near Mount Erebus or Mount Terror, I could find my way around.

There was something extraordinarily dramatic and tragic about the final Scott expedition, which we have recently seen reproduced on television. The heroic Britons, ill-equipped, toiled with agony through the snow and the ice, through mountain passes and piercing gales, and died at last so near relief—while at the same time Amundsen and his Norwegians, one gathers from his book, skied briskly and cheerfully to the Pole and back.

Scott failed, his heart told him, because though he reached the Pole he found Amundsen's flag already flying there. He died on the journey homeward. And now Byrd too, in spite of all his high achievements and honors, has just missed attaining completely the crown and apex of his career. He was in command of the U.S. Antarctic Expedition, which is our part of one of his life dreams—the great International Geophysical Year. But as his men entered the camp at the Pole he could not be with them; he lay dying in Boston, deprived at last even of the privilege of meeting his death on that grim Polar Continent he had learned to know so well.

Amundsen was more fortunate, for he died on a rescue expedition in the Arctic, seeking to save a man who was his enemy.

All stories from the Arctic and the Antarctic fill me with admiration of the hardihood and endurance of Norwegians, who, perhaps naturally, seem much better able than the rest of us to bear the cold and the darkness and the terrors of these regions of the ends of the earth.

There is, however, one little-known story of British gallantry which ranks with the best of the Scandinavians. This tale, *The Worst Journey in the World,* is told by Cherry-Garrard, one of the small group that went out from the Scott winter quarters to seek, for scientific purposes, eggs of the Emperor Penguins at a certain stage in their development. To secure them at this stage the men had to go in the dead of the antarctic winter night. The journey took them five weeks. It was a nightmare of Dante's "cold hell," with temperatures of sixty below zero. They did find the eggs of the Emperor Penguins, five of them, and in spite of appalling difficulties and suffering succeeded in returning alive to the expedition's winter quarters. His two comrades died later on the trip to the Pole, but Cherry-Garrard lived to carry the eggs to England.

When he got there he wrote to the Natural History Museum in South Kensington, London, that he was calling on a certain day, the sole survivor of the expedition, to deposit there the precious scientific fruits of the great adventure. But when he reached the door the custodian said, "I don't know nothing about no eggs; you'd best speak to Mr. Brown." Mr. Brown was occupied talking to a Person of Importance. Without a word of thanks he took the eggs and turned away. "I should like to have a receipt for the eggs, if you please," said the explorer. "It's not necessary," retorted Mr. Brown. "You needn't wait."

There are worse things than the bitter gales of the Antarctic!

Other tips of the earth also are fascinating, tips in another dimension—the summits of the highest mountains. When I was fourteen my family first visited Switzerland and stayed for some days at Zermatt. Gazing at the black, terrible, beautiful Matterhorn and reading that classic of mountaineering Edward Whymper's *Scrambles Amongst the Alps*, which describes the tragic first ascent of that mighty shaft of rock, my brother and I fell under the spell of the romance of Alpine climbing.

Ever after I followed with keen attention the gradual and painful conquest of the great peaks, until at last I stood with Hillary and Tenzing on Everest, the top of the world. The king of all sports, mountaineering!

"Look off beyond man's outermost footing into the unknown," I have written, but my examples of such reviving adventures of the mind have been only simple geographic ones on the surface of this our planet Earth. Choose your own tips, I recommend. If you prefer, as you probably will, to perch in your imagination on the Moon or Mars and gaze out into the frigid vastness of space, you will have an abundance of opportunities in the books of today. As for me, in my moments of relaxation I still find Attu more restful.

Besides my tip ends in space there are, happily for me, equally satisfying adventures of the mind in seeking tip ends of time—prehistory and archaeology. But the really great thrills of intellectual adventure on a higher plane, keying man to exaltation, lie, except for fragmentary and distant glimpses, beyond the scope of my knowledge and power. They come to the research scholar as he approaches the very tip ends of human knowledge in his field and realizes that he can perhaps throw a slim beam of light out into the darkness of ignorance that still encompasses mankind. I have often tried to conceive Einstein's sensations as this terrifying universe unrolled before him and he began to see the physical laws which direct its forces and powers. My own moments of scholarly perception and exaltation have been on a far humbler level. But as I approach the tip end of life itself I find that I can look out into the unknown reaches of eternity with something of my old eager sense of high adventure.